THE 419'S

a travelogue about a country on crack

Hatem Sabbagh

Copyright © 2016 Hatem Sabbagh-HATMANIA PUBLISHING

hatmaniapub@gmail.com

https://www.facebook.com/the419s/

Twitter: @the419s

Instagram: fouronenine419

All rights reserved.

ISBN: 9198325612
ISBN-13: 978-9198325614

This book is solely dedicated to Emilia, for seeing the best in me, before I even had a clue that the best in me even existed.

PROLOGUE

After 22 years in Sweden, I now reside and work in Nigeria. In the beginning, I didn't quite understand what was happening, or rather, I didn't think that my experiences later would be a part of my everyday life. I didn't think that it would be so incredibly fun that I would feel the urge to write notes as I went along, and that said notes would lead to this book. My notes soon became news letters that I sent to my beloved ones. They later became a blog, and finally a book. Thus the feeling in the texts, you will sense the transition and tag along. I'm no writer; I'm just a remarkably funny guy. Additionally, there will be tons of careless mistakes, horrible hyphenations, grammatic errors (this one is on purpose though), abbreviations, weird sentence structure and all kinds of oddities that could be perceived as I'm torturing the English language, things that would make Stephen Fry go nuts. The reason is not that I'm a floater as they say; it is to maintain the Nigerian feeling. You go to press with a half ass product, and you are proud of it, alternatively don't give a damn. And in true Nigerian/Lebanese spirit, you demand an extortionate amount of money for the big pile of crap.

These are my depictions from my perspective. To complicate matters, I am a multicultural nightmare. My father was Lebanese, and schooled from an early age in Germany. So Arabic stubbornness combined with a German sense of order is a big part of my life. I was born in Egypt (my mother is Egyptian), which is basically the worst of Africa and the worst of the Arab World. I grew up in Sweden and spent a better part of my adult life in Nigeria. This is just to inform you that my perspective is as strange as a perspective can be. However, it is how I view the world. And with a 150 million imaginative Nigerians, there has been no need whatsoever to spice things up. It is shocking and scandalous as it is.

There is a need for some clarification. Some facts are not correct anymore, as the book was written in 2010. The Vice-president later became President for example, the population has risen from 150 million to 180 million and so forth. Driving used to be an issue at the time, but not the same today. I will do my best to explain the changes along the way, but I might not be able to correct them all. Enjoy the story itself, instead of being a stickler. This book is not for the faint of heart; my depictions of the truth are sometimes harsh, cynical, judgmental and charged with guilt. Even flat out racist. But make no mistake; this is in no way a bible for the European far right. On the contrary, this book stems from a deep love, affection and respect for both Nigeria and its people. Before you pass judgement, think about this for a second. The country is kept together despite the fact that it has 180 million inhabitants, of which 80% lives under the UN poverty limit, 500 to 600 languages and 300 to 2000 tribes all depending on how you count. Also, big religion is part of daily life, to make matters even more complicated. And it´s intertribal. We can´t house supporters from two opposing soccer teams in the same bar without riots. They have avoided civil war since Biafra.

I would like to take this opportunity to thank everyone I know and a lot of people I don't know for their contributions.

Last but by no means least, this book would never have been written without the 150 million Nigerians that every day gave me heart attacks, fibrillation, high blood pressure and made me rip my hair, cry out of anger with their tricks, cons, scams and making sure that everything went **not** according to plan. So as we say in Pidgin "Omo, my ppl, a dey hail uo".

Despite all of this, my newly found brothers made me smile every day with their ingenuity and every time I thought I had the upper hand, they out played me. Oddly enough, they made me love Nigeria, despite me being able to list 1000 reasons to leave the place. When I'm not there, I miss it, even though I can't really give a single reason why. I guess it's as they say: Africa is like malaria, if it once enters your system it never leaves. Or as they say in Pidgin: "9ija dey fo bodyo" (I have Nigeria in my body i.e Nigeria is a part of me).

Stockholm/Abuja/Lagos

Autumn 2010/Spring 2016

THE 419'S-a travelogue about a country on crack

JANUARY 2009

I'm finally in Nigeria. I have landed in Kano, where the airport was an experience to say the least. At this specific moment though, everything is more or less a chock. Both positive and negative. Nothing is as I expected.

The country is to say the least different, and incredibly beautiful. It's very green, it's tropical, and the heat is dry, and not humid. The praise stops here though.

However it is every bit as chaotic as you can't imagine. The chaos started on the flight from Beirut. We traveled business class (I think MEA has the largest business class section I have ever seen, to Nigeria at least, but that is because Lebanese people refuse to fly coach, no matter if they can afford business class tickets or not, however, that is a different topic entirely). I sat next to a Nigerian who was wearing an Agbada (practically a dress) and a pair of new shiny havaianas. The best way to describe the dress is to quote Prince Philip (The Duke of Edinburgh) upon meeting the Nigerian President Obasanjo while he was wearing his Agbada. He looked at him and said "You look like you're ready for bed!" (He also replied to a journalists question on what his opinion was on Nigeria on his first visit with the fantastic phrase "I rather not say"). Anyways, my neighbor on the plane was drinking champagne while giving himself a thorough pedicure, by picking his toes whit all the force he could muster. Very much like a Saudi.

The airport was an experience in its own right. 25 men needed to be bribed because of all the weird rules, one of them included me needing a permission for my black bag ("we have regulations and there are procedures" as he said). Bullshit, of course, and two quid solved the problem. Some other guys on the airport used a more straight forward approach. A guy in customs stepped up to me, shook my hand as if I was his forgotten son, and introduced himself with the classic phrase "wettin you bring for me?" I quickly adapted and learned the proper meaning of that phrase. Basically it is translated to give me what I want and this will go by smoothly.

It seems I should have brought something with me, because within the first seventy hours, I have managed to get the same question from airport officials to the entire local payroll at the head office. It is topped with Happy New Year is well, which just adds to the urge and means something in the line of "you should have brought even more as usual".

The traffic is pure chaos. You always travel with locked doors, not because of risk of being kidnapped, but because you want to avoid people jumping into the car and not leaving unless they're getting paid. By people I mean primarily law enforcement.

You pee sitting down, on the spot you happen to occupy at the moment - for instance on the freeway. The women on the other hand pull up their skirt and pee standing. It's female liberation at its best.

People are very religious. In my short tenure I have met Jews, Christians, Muslims – you name it. Denominations that you have never heard of. Nigeria is the only country where Catholics marry 4 women at the same time, otherwise they will convert to Islam, which they honestly might do anyway. People change religion left, right and center, even though they are reading Bibles, the Koran, run to church - the works. Until shit hits the fan: the tribe goes before all else, the machetes are brought forth and they start

lynching each other. My college's driver was born a Muslim, but converted to Christianity because he could not read Arabic, but converted back again, upon learning Arabic.

Chichi works for me in the head office. Her task is simple but extremely important. Her job is to bring me coffee when I shout her name. I need a driver as well, apparently there is a driver with the name "Two-plus-two", and he will most probably be recruited, because of his amazing name. It's not the best of ideas for us to drive ourselves, you will learn why as you go along.

I was not feeling very well on my second day here, and made the mistake of asking where the closest hospital was. I got the reply "London". Apparently that is where we go if we are in need of medical evacuation. Sounds promising. Remains to be seen if I survive until my next post.

THE BEGINNING OF FEBRUARY 2009

These famous reports will hereinafter be referred to as the 419's.

I've got some news for you guys. I went shopping for necessities like detergent, toilet paper etc. It's obvious that the supermarkets here are for the expatriates and the few Nigerians who can afford them. It is horribly expensive.

I went to stock up on the essentials, and managed to rack up a bill equivalent to one I had in a Paris nightclub in my late twenties. At least if you look at price compared to the quality. In Nigeria, you can buy a drum set in the supermarket btw. That's good to know, isn't it?

On the shopping list: Detergent, soap, milk, bug spray, cockroach spray, flour, cheese, bread and eggs. 170 pounds - a great bargain.

The cheese went for almost 25 pounds. To prevent me from nicking it, I had to pay for it in the deli counter instead of at the register.

When I was done shopping I tried to leave the supermarket like you do in the western world. Apparently this was a huge mistake, and I was wrestled to the floor by two huge and very angry security guards. After the commotion (which to be honest scared the living hell out of me, as I thought I was becoming a victim of a gang rape at first). Apparently the procedure is to voluntarily submit yourself to getting strip searched by the guards before leaving, then have your receipt and goods scrutinized in order to make sure you haven't been shoplifting.

Buying guns here is easier than buying cheese. Goods that we are used to is hard currency, if you find something you like you have to empty the entire shelf. This nearly bankrupts you, but you cannot imagine what extremes you go to for a taste like home.

Speaking about food, I made some inquiries about the wildlife, but apparently the animal life has been decimated. Why? They eat everything that moves. It's called bush meat. I have tried it twice and you never know what you'll get (meaning what animal) - you eat first and ask questions later. This is just because I am still a newbie. So basically I go with don't ask don't tell when it comes to what I eat. Just so I don't regurgitate afterwards. I've had the honor to try python and beaver. Python was a real highlight, beaver as well. But it was apparently upper class bush meat. Real bush meat is road kill. But, I will need to be more integrated before I go there.

I have seen a lot of monkeys. My cousin has a monkey in our compound in Auchi. He bought it for two pounds. In other words you get twelve monkeys for the price of one cheese and you have one pound to spare.

We have just been informed that we will host a party in our compound the coming week. The Vice-president at the time, (who later became President) and a couple of ministers have arranged the party, without really asking us. We are counting on an orgy in liquor and loose women of course, and that the bill will be sent to us. A lesser renovation will be needed after they trash the place. Our Managing Director who is from Germany, is not very happy about the party; it doesn't go hand in hand with his sense of order.

A new insight is that our tax expert is royalty. A King basically. After doing some research, it turns out that Nigeria, as the republic that it is, proudly hosts over 250 000 Kings. HRH Chief Ukwu is the bomb. His Royal Highness is the subordinate of our CFO Mr. Baron, which makes the conversations sound ridiculous.

HRH Chief Ukwu: "Mr., Baron I need to leave earlier on Monday, is that possible?"

Mr. Baron: "Your Royal Highness, this is not a day care center where you can waltz in and out as you please, you are staying put on Monday!"

You get the point.

As I told you before, our Chairman is from Auchi. I met his daughter yesterday, a really nice girl that really wanted to introduce me to her siblings. Apparently there are 36 of them. And an additional 5 that are adopted (I mean just in case, so the family is not too small). I have met an estimate of five to seven of them by now. There is just not enough time.

I had a trip up north the other day. To an extremely isolated village. I was greeted by the villagers residing close to our project. A couple of them where butt naked. I am, well, blessed to put in those terms, but from a European point of view. But these guys, they could give John Holmes an inferiority complex. Now, I thought they walked around as God brought them to the world, just to brag. Or because of restraint on their budgets. But I was wrong. Apparently they are legally insane as the term goes, or just insane. And that is how the other villagers know that they are nuts, and it helps the villagers stay as far away from them as humanly possible. Not a bad solution.

I've also realized the importance of warning triangles. When (not if) you have an accident, you run away with a machete and chop down parts of a tree that you toss out on the road, like a warning. Now the cars coming from behind, will instead of hitting your car, hit one of the logs you put in the middle of the road as a warning and go down the ditch that way. Much safer.

I submitted my passport in order to extend my visa. My nosy driver couldn't keep his hands to himself and starting going through my passport, and quickly realized I was born in Cairo, meaning to him - I'm African. This has meant that invitations to circumcisions, weddings, funerals etc. have rained down on me since Monday. For now though, I cannot handle more nudity. We will see what the future holds.

Being new in Nigeria and speaking about chock, cannot be done really without addressing the language. Well it's not a language really, its Pidgin English, but still. Now, before you go to Nigeria, you are under the impression that everybody speaks English. Which is correct. But, it's far from the Queens English. And, to make matters worse, it sounds like English, it smells like it, it even feels like it. But in the end, it's gibberish.

It's Ebonics basically. And it's really lingua franca. This is the kind of social awkwardness that arise.

I had a meeting with a person and upon arriving the following conversation unfolded when I informed his secretary that he was expecting me:

Secretary: He don't go.

Me: Perfect, tell him that I arrived (In my best Sky Channel/BBC accent).

Secretary: No sa (Sir), you don't andastand (understand), he don't go"

Me: I do understand, he has not left, so inform him I am here, so we can get on with it.

We went on like that, back and forth, for a couple of minutes until I just lost it and left.

After some research I reached the conclusion that "He neva go" means that he is still around in Pidgin. "He don go" means he has left. I think this is a mix up from the understanding of the use of the word don't from the British "You don't say". It makes sense now. But there and then. O lord, my anger knew no limits.

MID FEBRUARY 2009

A few more days have passed and I have stocked up on new experiences and stories.

I've had the honor to try "Kilichi" today. It's some kind of meat snack made from meat, beaten down to the size of an A4 paper and bombarded with some kind of strong chili. It's not bad at all. However it is really twice the chili experience. Chili in, chili out. Both extremities was on fire.

We've also found the weirdest church:

The Jewish, Zionist, Christian Catholic Church of Jesus Christ of Palestine.

A pretty strange combo. If you don´t understand why, you should brush up on your theology.

I've also gotten a taste of Nigerian efficiency. I had finished a document and submitted it for copying here at the office. Everything was in order, 100 pages nice and tidy.

What I got back was 4 stapled copies, completely helter-skelter. Some pages were upside down, other without text on the front. He had taken a good amount of time in order to make it such a mess. He got a quick scolding and then we finished it as you do in Nigeria: Sorryo. Which kind of gives you the sense that the entire issue is solved, from the man apologizing's perspective at least. Highly unsatisfying for me I might add.

Apparently I am not the only one who hates this approach. My hatred is shared by an Italian that works for us who got his leg crushed because somebody decided not to follow the security protocol, and topped it off with a sorryo after dismembering the poor guy.

Customs has a message, not only for us, but also for mankind. We've got some construction equipment here that hasn't been cleared through customs due to a mistake on our part. I tried to fix it yesterday; since we don't want our import license revoked, I called the customs and explained the situation. The official in charge at the customs office told me: "don't wake a sleeping bear" and ended the call by slamming the phone shut in my ear. The problem is still unsolved both for us and the customs. It´s lose-lose. So I guess the bear is still sleeping? I have no clue what he meant to be honest, and how it applies.

We were out on a drunken binge this Saturday, but let's save that for the next update.

After my initial encounter with Pidgin English, I wanted nothing to do with it. But with time, my fascination has grown more for each passing day. It makes sense, in an African way. And it´s highly vivid and alive. So,

I will enlighten you with my new understanding of Pidgin (limited as it is at this stage):

A don close = basically means that I am shutting down, so I can leave/I'm done for the day.
Chop = Eat.
Sorryo = my deep apology (Stop yelling at me).
Ide around = He is here.
Ide not around = He is not here.
Wettin de happon = what's up/How are you doing, literally what is happening.
He don collo = He has gone mad/He is crazy.
No wahala = No problem
Pepe no res = I have no money.

A don close.

A NICE DAY IN MARCH 2009

Packaging! It's easy to go blind in Africa, but I have made a discovery that should've been put into the spotlight in the first letter. Of course, you can't drink the water; you have to buy it in stores. You put water in plastic bags and peanuts in glass bottles. In general, that is the best and easiest way to the describe Nigeria as a whole in one sentence. "Water in plastic bags and peanuts in glass bottles". Maybe they should use it as their slogan in the UN? Or to attract tourists? But in general it is Alice in wonderland. What works here, would never work, or be appropriate, or even moral/legal outside these borders.

Nigeria has 150 million people and everyone has 3 telephones each. I've always wondered why, and I've finally received an answer. To receive text messages, you have to call yourself now and then for the texts to get through. The reason is apparently that the country has a capacity of 50 million lines, but has sold about 200 million subscriptions. It goes without a saying that the network doesn't work great, so you have to have one subscription from every mobile phone provider.

I experienced a local funeral that was as much upside down as everything else here. It reminded more of an American spring break celebration, with drunkenness, vomit, party hats, euphoria and intercourse everywhere.

Yesterday, we had a visitor from Beirut. 30 minutes later the driver called. He was very frustrated, as he couldn't find the lady visiting us. We found out that he had been sitting with the sign in his lap, in the car in the parking lot. Not very strange that he couldn't find her.

I also experienced my first cheque fraud. The wrong company name, falsified signatures and a horribly counterfeited cheque, with the correct account number which led to a pretty large payment from our account. The fraud was of such a low quality that it makes you wonder how they managed to withdraw funds from the account. Well, it helps if the bank branch manager is in on it I guess.

We are not allowed to use our credit cards in ATM machines, on the internet or in stores. The only thing that will happen if your credit card leaves your pocket is that they will be skimmed.

This Saturday I was at a bush bar called Monsters Inc. It consisted mostly of planks in the bush supported by two fridges. They were serving lukewarm beer, and the ambiance consisted mostly of humidity, mosquitos and African women trying to get you in bed using brute force, while still making you pay. The Brits and Germans seemed to like it.

Nowadays, I'm an African for real. I have been infected with malaria, and will live with it for the rest of my life. I visited our company doctor, Dr. Hasan from Pakistan: as tall as Mrs. Pepperpot. His remedies are the same no matter the disease: blue pills, green pills, yellow pills and plenty of ice cream.

In most countries you will get salmonella from the water or raw chicken. Here, you have to be alert when eating vegetables. They have to be rinsed in some kind of chlorine, and sometimes even that doesn't help. I have managed to be infected as well, and had to visit Dr. Hasan again. The remedy? Blue pills, green pills, yellow pills and plenty of ice cream.

I will end today's report with more Pidgin English. This language keeps fascinating me. In many ways, it is a language in its own right. It is really an African vernacular. And it reflects the logic in many ways. Why have different words for being a thief, and stealing, when using the word "tief" can work instead of both. Nigerians are very good at preserving energy, they never do more than necessary, so it makes complete sense. I am mesmerized, the more I learn, the more eager I get. So, again, time for more Pidgin English:

Dash = So basically a dash stems from the Portuguese word *dache*, and means gift or tribute. The Nigerian journalist Peter Enahoro gives a very accurate description of this phenomenon in his book "How to be a Nigerian". A dash is not tips, because tips are based on a job well done that can be evaluated. And not a bribe, because a bribe is subject to the return of a favor. A dash, is an incentive. It´s not conditioned, given before the actual task is done with no control of the outcome. Basically you are paying to grease the wheel, but without knowing how it will go. Most probably into the black hole the dash is.
Oyibo = White man, or literally: man without skin.
Fresh fish = Newcomer to Nigeria (easy to fool).
JJC= Same as above. Johnny Just Came.
Oga = Boss.
Oga Patapata= The biggest of bosses.
Acting big man=When your second brushes up, and acts like the big boss when you are not around.
Go by leg/trek = Walk.
Go come = Please come again, or "have a nice trip".
Carry am go = Take this thing to that place.
Pick am carry am go = Put that shit back where it came from.
NEPA = Nigerian Elecitrical Power Authority, more commonly known as Never Expect Power Always.
Na be so = Isn't that so?
A-be/Abi = Don't you agree?
Abi na wettin?=What is it?
Go slow = Traffic jam.
Niash = Ass, or a more correct translation is booty.
On it = Turn it on
Off it= Turn it off (This can sometimes be misused by white men who pretend to speak Pidgin, or think they do. "I will wear a tie, and if it's too hot I will off it" which in their minds translates to removing it.)
Bros = Brother
How na?= How are you doing?

Shake body = Have sex, would you like to dance, or can we please pay the bill, all depending on the context.
A beg = Can I please have/Could you please.
Omo=My Child/children.
Mosquito= Prostitutes by night, in a bar/nightclub environment.
Butterfly= Prostitutes by day, on the beach.

Now that we have learned a couple of words, let's try out some sentences.

Nepa done die abi? = The electricity has been shut down again right?

Bros, who carry u go there? = My brother who sent you there/to that place/took you there?

Nobody carry me, na me carry ma self go or Nobody carry me go, a go go carry my self come= This is where it starts to become complicated, but that means nobody sent me there, I went there by myself. The second version is starting to dig deep. And makes it nearly impossible for a newbie to understand what is going on.

Abeg-o make a shake body = If this is said in a restaurant, after a meal, you are asking for the bill. Which basically means to be shaken while held upside down to empty ones pockets.

GETTING A DRIVER'S LICENCE

I received my driver's license today, two hours after applying for it. I didn't need to submit anything or even translate my Swedish driver's license. I just filled in an application, where I made the mistake to write that I had a B driver's license (here you use the letter E for some reason). The guy in charge gave me a scolding that could be heard across the country: it's apparently not up to me to decide what I can drive. So he asked me one control question: can you drive a car? I said: yes. He said: good.

I'm now sitting with my Nigerian driver's license in my hands, and I can legally drive a 3.5 ton truck. I've never driven one before, and I'm definitely not going to start here. Additionally, I had to submit my blood type. It has to be printed on the license in case of an accident. Of course, they got that wrong too.

I've also received my "hunting license", meaning I'm now allowed to bear arms; shotguns and AK 47's. Africa beware.

They have pretty cool names here. I told you in an earlier part about "Two-plus-two". They also seem to have a fondness for weekdays. Monday, Tuesday, Wednesday, Thursday, Friday, Saturday, Sunday. I thought it was cool until I met a guy called Today. Talk about being affirmative.

My hairdresser is a big, bald black man. He's 2 meters tall, with a body that would put Arnold Schwarzenegger to shame. Bimbo is of course his name.

I opened a bank account for the company. The form is not exactly like that of Barclays Bank:

- Date of marriage (ETA if you are single)
- Favorite color
- Favorite sport
- Favorite person in sports
- Wife/girlfriend email address
- Club membership
- Number of kids and their names
- Favorite airline
- Favorite author
- Hobbies
- Favorite music (highlife, gospel, jazz, other)
- Your nickname

Makes no sense.

Let's conclude once again with some Pidgin. Today we will have a look at the grammar and compare with English. A bit more of an academic approach, if you so will. This is from a thesis of some sort, that I found many years ago, unfortunately I am not able to find it again, and credit the proper source.

A de kom = "I am coming or I usually come"
A go de kom = "I will be coming or I will continue/make a habit of coming"

A dọn de kọm = "I have/had started coming"

A go dọn de kọm = "I will have started coming"

A dọn kọm = "I have come/arrived"

A go dọn kọm = "I will have come/arrived"

Action verbs:
Tif don tek wi moni = A thief has taken our money.
Jon don kom fo wi haos. = John has come to our house.
Jon don silip fo chie. = John has slept on the chair
Stative verbs:
Meri don get plenty money. = Mary has had much money; i.e. Mary has become rich.
Dem don no se wi don go. = They have known that we have gone.
Di pikin don fain. = The child has fine; i.e. The child has become fine.

MAY 1ST (LABOUR DAY) - 2009

At the time of writing this, it was the first of May. Of course, I went to march with my fellow labourers as is the tradition in Sweden. But this was my first march ever. Not because I'm some kind of champagne socialist, but because for once, I could identify with the labourers message:

Same Job – Equal Bribes.

BLOWING MY OWN HORN

The following took place during the end of May 2009.

It's time again. I've been away for a while, with little to no internet access. I've been to Warri -
The Mecca of Kidnapping!

To go to Warri, you have to be equipped with the Mopol (Mobile Police), meaning an armed cop in every car (asleep but still), loads of guns in the car and military escort.

The roads in the bush are complete garbage and sometimes impossible to traverse. The trip takes 12 hours, and luckily our jeep is equipped with dvd and TV.

There are many military check points on the way down, where you are greeted with phrases like "Happy Sunday" (on a Wednesday). It should come as no surprise to you by now that this means "pay up, or stay put."

We took a small detour on the way to Warri, and passed through Onitsha. Now to cross the Niger River, you have to cross the Onitsha Bridge. The bridge was completed in the 60´s by the French, and has been highly trafficated since. It carries ten times more load then it is constructed for. It is as scary as you can imagine to cross. You can actually feel the bridge moving under you. Anyway that is another topic all together. Now the Bakassi Boys rule Onitsha. It is a local youth vigilante group that are extremely violent, and enjoy plenty of local support. The thing is, where they rule there is order. They are fierce on crime, well more than fierce, it´s flat out human rights violations. Bruce Willis-Die Hard style. Yippikiyaye motherfucker-style. But it works.

Two drunk guys decided to ambush us as we were just leaving the bridge for the mainland. They were a bit too drunk to notice the Bakassi Boys "military" (I use the term rather loosely, it´s more a Lord of war-like militia) check point.
The entire attack took less than a minute to quash. They threw two truck tires over both of them, which basically makes you stand in your place without being able to move, for a limited amount of time at least. Poured gasoline over them, and lit them on fire while giving us a thumbs up/you are clear to pass eye-contact. I gave them my lighter, I mean, it´s the least I could do.

After our excursion we decided to send the cars beforehand and fly back to Abuja. Not the best of ideas in hindsight. Upon my arrival to Warri's airport (I think it was voted as one of the worst in the world, or the neighboring one in Port Harcourt with Abuja and Lagos on the

THE 419'S-a travelogue about a country on crack

bottom 10-list as well, 30% of the world's worst airports for one country is not a bad feat, at all) it dawned on me that Warri´s airport consists of a whole lot of nothing. A large tarpaulin over a semi steel structure instead of hangar, no tarmac, basically, a landing strip in the bush. Upon boarding the plane, I noticed something extremely disturbing. The plain had a flat tire, so I called on the captain.

After informing him of my discontent for the situation, he looks at me like I am an idiot and says in Pidgin:

"Oga, we na go drive na, we go flyo". Meaning: "We are not going drive, we are going to fly."

So, after digesting this fantastic statement, I decided to drive back, without security. The choice was easy for me, a possible kidnapping or certain death.

My 419's have gotten some traction down here, and everyone feel like they want to contribute with some material. So we had a sit down the other day in the compound canteen.

I broke the ice with something that happened to me recently. But first, some background to put you in the story. I work for my cousin who is in his seventies and two years younger than my father. He went to Nigeria in the 60´s and met a Nigerian illiterate man and they decided to become partners. Both were flat out broke. 40 years later this fruitful relationship is still going strong, and employs around 25-40000 people across 30 companies. What makes it even more interesting is that these two are flat out the two most eccentric people on the planet, with quirks you can´t imagine. Donald Trump is mellow in comparison. One of the reasons why I got sacked by the way was that I was considered to be too eccentric. Which says quite a lot about me I guess.

One quirk, shared across the board between my cousin and his partner, and puts the whole conglomerate in a frenzy is red apples from Lebanon.

They get delivered to the head office, on Tuesdays. They fly business class to Kano, and from there a five hour bus ride to Abuja. Upon reaching the head office the cost of transportation increases the price of the apples to the equivalent of their weight in diamonds.

Upon reaching the head office, our HR department, in liaison with the procurement department counts the inventory and prepares an excel spread sheet. This sheet gets distributed to key stake holders in management and all hell breaks loose. Everybody argues on the amount of apples needed and to whom they should be sent. Speaker of the house should get 4, the deputy senate president gets 1 apple. Depending on the issues of the day that needs to be promoted. After the cock fight, the sheet reaches my cousin for final editing. After he edits it another cock fight takes place. Until we settle on the final version. This spectacle, involves at least 15-20 people, with six figure salaries (on the higher end) and takes a day. It´s an absolute waste of money and time. And highly political (internally). We spend the rest of the week regrouping and building alliances for the next shipment.

My cousin's partner who is our Chairman by the way, is highly involved in this as well. Not the bickering. He wants just wants his share of apples.

Ghassan or Gus, decides to contribute as well. One day Gus is on the way to his car, and notices that the windows are down, and there is plenty of towels inside the car. He doesn't reflect really and takes a seat. Upon sitting down, he notices that the entire car is soaking wet on the inside. He asks the driver what had happened - apparently, he was washing the car with the windows open.

Peter pitched in with a story about his driver. Apparently Peter noticed that the car needed to be filled up with oil about once a month. This is mightily suspicious, so he decided to monitor the whole situation. After a couple of weeks, he noticed that his driver stole the oil from the vehicle and sold it to an *aboki* as we say. An *aboki* is a northerner most probably a Muslim, who offers the service of lubricating stuff with used oil. So, Peter, did the only right thing. He told to driver to stop stealing, and gave him an additional 20 pounds to cover what the theft brought in. After 4 months, his driver came back with 80 pounds and told him "Sir, I don't want the money, keep them, just let me steal the oil instead". Amazing.

It has also come to our attention that the family's inner circle have nicknames so that our local employees can bad mouth us without repercussion. My cousin and I managed to get hold of some of the nicknames by threatening his maid with a sword.

My cousin, the founder: Original Master. This has its base that many "masters" have come and left, and he is always around, in one way or the other.
His wife: Iron Lady/Barbed Wire, she is no push over, tuff as nails.
My other cousin: Good Boy, completely random (it was us who used the sword to get the nick names).
My cousin's brother in law: Iron fist, he is incredibly cheap, and never releases more money than necessary.
My third cousin (our CFO): Superglue, he is even cheaper. He went ape shit once, upon reviewing the books of one of our construction projects. They spent £ 7 000 on "printing material" in a month. "We are building a road, not a printing press!" It was hilarious. He lost it on all levels.

I want to conclude with a nice cinematic experience that occurred in Warri.

We were supposed to watch Transporter 3. We made it through half the movie, and then the piece of crap decided to shut down. Apparently, they had a slight technical error… no electricity. What's a huge problem? Cinema on fire?

SLOWLY TURNING BUSH (SOMETIME IN AUGUST 2009)

I have to start by admitting that I haven't written any 419's lately because I, to my big surprise, have turned "Bush", as we call it. In other words, I've become completely indifferent to everything that's going on around me. Everything here has become part of my daily life; I don't notice the crazy stuff or even raise an eyebrow. In two weeks I will be picking my toes as I'm drinking champagne, or change religion more often than I'm changing my underwear.

What triggered me to write again was me reading the blogs and travel journals of two other people. It made me get a grip, and see the country with reinvigorated eyes in order to keep bringing you entertainment and, most of all, a little glimpse into how Africa works. Without being politically correct.

So let's skip the foreplay and go straight into the nitty-gritty.

One thing that should be brought into attention is the fact that I haven't seen ONE SINGLE speed limit sign since I got here. At least not in the capital. I've come across a few on the countryside but here, there are no signs to be seen. It's in line with Nigeria's answer to zero tolerance policy. No one shall survive in traffic.

Let's keep talking about traffic. In Nigeria, they are incredibly time efficient; so much so that they don't give a damn about using the existing bridges when crossing the freeways, instead they bash their way over the lanes on the freeway. Two months ago, a guy stepped into the road, giving an incoming truck driver about one meter to stop. The guy got smashed, and an angry lynch mod was created before anyone could blink. Of course, the truck driver had no chance to stop whatsoever. 30 tons at an arm's length is impossible. It happened again yesterday, this time I shrugged my shoulders like it was normal.

To make driving a vehicle more of a sport, the Nigerians like to surprise each other by walking over the road in the middle of the night. The fact that there are no lights and that they are darker than the average man doesn't seem to stop anyone, instead it seems like it is beneficial to the adventure. The best thing you can do is to blink with your headlights; they will stop like a scared deer, much like the expression. Luckily, having experience from Swedish driving, you have a natural, ingrained behavior from slippery roads; you always drive like you're driving behind wild animals, not in front of them. I'm cruising past people without an issue. For you people that have a hard time keeping up, I have begun driving a bit now and then and developed these skills along the way.

Another detail that fits nicely into these stories are the cannibals in Calabar. There is a tribe there that still enjoys the delicacy that is human meat. This, of course, is highly illegal. The tribes in Calabar brushes it off as urban legends, but it is very much real, but under the counter trade. Like buying Cohibas in LA. One of our MD's that can be described as a "bigger model" (fat like a pig). Being that big is considered a good thing, something that imposes authority. People like me don't impose the same kind of authority like a big old Cheltenham beer belly. Anyway, he got a visit by the community chief in Calabar.

Anyway, after the visit, they insisted on lunch. The fat guy got the flattering title "Sweat Meat", which in his ears sounded like they respected him and that he was going to be honored with a proper meal. He was delighted by the invitation. I had to take him aside. I'm hungry, the fat guy said, and they call me sweat meat. I looked at him with a stern look, they're saying that you are sweat meat - we are the lunch, you moron.

Difficult things to put into a job description. But that is part of my daily operational routine.

THIS IS THE LAST OF THE OLD 419's

It's time again! Today, we will begin with a rough a la carte menu. I have yet again eaten bush meat.

On today's menu:

Four o Four, or Jay Five as it's called, meaning a four wheel drive, or five if you count the tail. You got that right, I've eaten dog, and some palm wine to ease it down with.

Dog is great stuff, really great. Palm wine on the other hand kind of reminds me of fermented piss. It ferments and grows in your mouth. A horrible experience. Much like pidgin, at first. Once you get used to it, it's amazing, especially the distilled stuff. It's African champagne basically. Or bush champagne is more accurate.

I must say though, dog will be definitely be savored again, both as a pet and as lunch.

I told you earlier about our tax expert that just so happens is a King as well. I mean that in all aspects. Chief Ukwu arrives at noon and goes home a couple of hours later. He walks around bare foot and is always drunk.
Yesterday, he was working overtime. The time was something like 7pm and I thought he had left the lights on in his office. I walk in to shut the lights off, and quickly realize how naive I am. Chief Uku has brought in

some 20 year old girl that he is screwing on the desk, and instead of canceling the activity, he looks back and gives me the thumbs up. I don't know what to say.

The infidelity and drunkenness of Chief Ukwu is not exactly appreciated by his wife. When he was living on the compound, he usually came home late, ending in heated arguments with his wife. One night when shit really hit the fan, the mopol woke up from all the yelling. In his sleepy state, he did the only right thing; he emptied his machine gun into the air, waking the entire compound causing panic as they thought they were under attack. The Chief had to leave the camp immediately, and his wife left him just as fast. No cause for concern for the Chief though, he still has three wives left.

The newspapers are busy today, writing about the unrest in northern Nigeria. It's not the usual suspects causing havoc over the oil in the delta – this time it's the religious groups that suddenly decided to decrease the population, simply by increasing the death-rate.

In the south, they want the oil-filled delta to become an independent country. Not to anyone's surprise, they have grown tired of everyone stealing their stolen oil money; you have to fight for your right to keep what you steal!

They have been the source of chaos for 10 years, blowing up pipelines, kidnapping people and ships. Mostly blowing pipelines though. They have heard the expression "it's in the pipeline" too many times when they have asked if they're getting their own country. Apparently, they took that literally and decided to find out what really was hiding in these pipes. A very good joke, which they made up themselves. They told us that when we had dinner with them the other day. Nice guys.

The government issued a raid against them a couple of weeks ago. They confiscated loads of weapons, listing them in the newspaper:
- AK47's
- Rocket launchers
- Voodoo dolls

There you go. We are safe. The voodoo dolls are confiscated.

ANTELOPE RALLY-TIME TO UNRAVEL THE CONCEPTS

There are a couple of concepts that need to be unraveled in order for this story to make sense. Antelopes and Gazelles. Of course, we're not talking about Safari – we are talking about women. Antelopes are Nigerian women selling themselves, not to the highest bidder, but the first bidder. A bit like an auction without competition or a man swinging his gavel. The drawback with antelopes, apart from the risk of HIV, is that they're never the complete package. Best case scenario, they are looking less than okay but with one nasty drawback (if you ignore the fact that they sell themselves).

Gazelles on the other hand, are like Naomi Campbell. They are not easy to find, even harder to get. Hence the name.

Now for the concept of an antelope rally. When I was in Lagos, I met two Englishmen that were a bit older than me. I dare say that they were both very good looking (not better than me, of course). They were conducting antelope rallies. An antelope rally is all about keeping your cool as you're picking hookers for each other. You have to take the ugliest one, you have to have sex with them and your buddy has to pay. The drawback is, of course, that you have to have sex with the ugliest girls in the joint. It can sound something like this:

> -Oh, you get that one, she looks like a black Saddam Hussein, nice moustache.
> -Fuck, you saw her first.
> -Yeah lucky me, go ahead, ask how much.

A couple of minutes pass, and then a girl that looks enters the room. The Saddam Hussein lookalike suddenly feels like a Ford model.

The guy who chose Saddam for his friend says:

-Motherfucker, I should have kept my cool.
-Jackpot, she's all yours.

In the midst of all this chaos, dealing and negotiations, these nutjobs ask me:

-Hatem, don't you want join our game?
-I will pass.

It's not really my thing to sleep with one of the three ugliest girls here, and then pay for it. It's as I say, I don't pay for sex, and I get paid. On top of that, I don't have jungle fever. I have a weakness for blonds and brunettes.

My question as to why you pay for this kind of madness: why do you want the worst there is, and pay for it on top?

Say what you will, but these guys are more broken than the average man. And yes, they are married with children. Nice.

THE TIP OF MY PENIS

Once and for all, let's debunk this thing they say about African men. Are they better equipped than the average man?

To help us investigate this, I have a couple of stories that make this post not only factual but straight up scientific.

Let's start with exhibit 1. Not entirely unexpected, it's about yours truly. Yours truly thinks that he can stand tall (no pun intended) compared to other westerners.

Yours truly learned the hard way (again-no pun intended) that this is nothing to be proud of. I was sleeping on my back, naked, with morning glory giving me a couple of extra inches to boot. I dare say that you're at your largest in the morning. We are talking about the size of an average dwarf here.

THE 419'S-a travelogue about a country on crack

Without warning, the maid bashes into the room, with my flagpole standing tall. She puts her hand over her mouth and starts giggling. Of course, my first reaction is that she was embarrassed by the whole scenario, but as she leaves the room, I can hear her "whispering": "Ahah, dat ting dey smallo". This is my first point that supports my theory that the competition here is fierce.

Exhibit 2: This one happened when we were renovating the compound. Our idiot of a project manager thought it was a very intelligent idea to let the local employees shower on the compound, without really building any showers. So they used what they had, a hose basically and showered butt naked in front of well, every Tom, Dick and Harry. Worried married men approached management pleading and begging for the removal of the showers or at least to build some walls.
My cousin, who has a very bad temper decided to lose it and instead of fixing the problem attack marriage as an institution with the argument:

   -Do you think your wife will start to sleep with them?

Obviously quite impressed by his witty comment, my cousin put on a grin. He was not ready for an even wittier response though.

   -It's not that she will have sex with them, she has stopped having sex with me.

Exhibit 3: This story is dedicated to our dear friend Nicholas Dawaliby (some curiosa: his last name is Arabic for car tire), that goes by the nickname Hajj. Hajj had just came home from Beirut during Christmas break and a Stephen, one of our local employees that works in the accounting department, was kind enough to ask him how his break was. He answered, and to be polite, he asked the guy the same question back.

The answer he got:

"I got an infection on the tip of my penis", going into detail about how he thought it happened, what it looked like, the side effects and so on. At the same time he was making gestures with his hand to show that he was talking about "the tip of my penis".

Hajj was in chock over the disgusting nature of the topic, but just as he started getting used to the subject, he realized what was truly the matter for concern. He was staring at his hand and the gestures he was making, and realized that what was "the tip of my penis" to this guy was the whole penis to most of us. Stephen was using his index and middle finger to show that it was "the tip of my penis".

I rest my case. Everything is huge in Africa, even the phone numbers are way too long.

An American study (Journal of Urology) determined in 1996 that an average penis is 12.9 centimeters. Thinking about the sizes you encounter in Africa, I have reached the conclusion that the Chinese and Indians are shrinking the world average.

I was in Beijing a couple of years ago, and was having a drink with a Swedish politician. In order to avoid scandal I will keep his name to myself. He noticed that I was running to the toilet all the time, and raised the question. Now, I never use the urinal. It's a concept that I don't understand, you basically pee into others people pee, while splashing yourself and the others next to you, while engaging in conversation. However in China, that was the only thing I used. Because, as I told my friend, that this is only about power. It's a show of force. And for once, I am the Nigerian.

A BIT UNDER THE WEATHER

Today I'm not in the mood to write. I'm a bit under the weather as I'm having a cold.

I'm going to give orders and yell at the locals. It makes me feel colonial, and imperial, and that always puts me in a good mood.

FLYING DOMESTICALLY

Flying domestically is as cool as everything else in Nigeria.

First of all, the airlines are using cool slogans that of course have no relationship to reality:
ARIK – Wings of Nigeria.

THE 419'S - a travelogue about a country on crack

Virgin – Very Virgin, Very Nigerian.

A lot of buzzwords and empty phrases. ARIK should be called Broken Wings of Nigeria, but you get it the gist of it.

When traveling domestically in Nigeria, you first have to go to the terminal for domestic flights. This is the number one newbie mistake. Every domestic flight departs from that terminal, except the ARIK flights that depart from the international terminal.

Additionally, the check-in desk is squeezed into a corner next to the toilets, and the security is performed at a table that you usually see at exhibitions.

The next thrilling experience felt almost cartoonish. After circulating for an hour over Lagos airport, the pilot grabs the mic and says:
"Ladies and gentlemen, at last we can start the landing process; the control tower is no longer on fire."

Exactly what you want to hear as a passenger.

Last but not least, we conclude with another cartoonish story that took place almost a year ago. A one hour flight took place like 800 meters above ground. Every hut, shed on the way was of course demolished by the turbulence.

Upon landing, the captain decided to share the following nugget to his passengers.

> -Thank God we managed this flight, although we had a crack in the front window.

Fantastic!

"LET THE FEET DO THE TALKING" - LARS LAGERBÄCK

As you probably know, the qualifiers to the world cup of soccer were held about 5 months ago. Not that I know or care, someone told me. I've never cared about soccer, I have a hard time seeing the charm in 22 sweaty overpaid idiots chasing a little piece of plastic.

Anyway, to make a short story long, as my good friend Ivan always says, or as I say about him, the Nigerian team was on route to qualify to the world cup. One of the Nigerian governors was very concerned about this. He addressed the media and said just that: "I'm concerned", and started calling a couple of other governors to figure out how they could solve this. I can't tell you the names of the governors, due to security reasons. Said and done, after a short while all the other governors where on board, met, and came to the conclusion that the best course of action was to start a "presidential task force", with the sole purpose to help the Nigerian team (Super Eagles I think they call themselves) to advance to the world cup.

Governor X went as far as setting up a fund, and funding it. Soon all the other governors followed suit. In less than a week, the committee had about £50 million to their disposal.

The news spread like wildfire across the nation, and soon the president held a speech to the nation George Bush style with the title and message: "I am also concerned", where he agreed with the governors, gave credit to their work and wanted to show his support by hosting a banquet to further discuss how to help the "Super Eagles" advancing.

At the same time as this was happening, the Nigerian team was fighting like shmucks without getting a dime from these governors, not one ball, no new shoes, nothing.

Said and done, the banquet was held by the "concerned" president that once again gave credit to the governors, and right there they came up with a solution how to help the team, to the sound of a standing ovation I might add. In order to help the team, they decided that they would use the money to buy first class flight tickets to all the governors, and their families (note that a first class ticket to South Africa cost something like £10.000), 5 star hotels and tickets to all the games, including the final. The jubilation knew no bounds.

Approximately at the same time, the national team advanced without any help from "the presidential task force", but the team still gave thanks to the president et al for helping them and giving them their support.

THE 419'S - a travelogue about a country on crack

At this stage, they had spent about 49 out of the 50 million pounds, so they had about 1 million left. There were talks about bringing in Sven-Göran Eriksson, but as you all know he has a weakness for blondes and brunettes, so there wasn't much for him in Nigeria. You wouldn't be able to spot Svennis at an antelope rally, so to speak. Lagerbäck on the other hand is, apparently, and he could muster getting there for the measly price of one million pounds.

Said and done, Lagerbäck signs the contract, and is housed in Hilton Abuja. This place has by the way been compared to something else by a Swedish bureaucrat when he got upgraded to a suite. With wall-to-wall carpets and a gas stove, he allegedly said:

"This feels like a fucking white trash trailer"

Anyway, let's fast forward to the press conferences, were media from all over the world are gathered in a media-frenzy. 400 journalists, all dressed for success, and then Lagerbäck, dressed in Adidas sweatpants and a Nigerian national team t-shirt. The T-shirt is two sizes to small, and makes him look like a green sausage. Or an obese leprechaun.

You have to understand one thing about Nigeria. Protocol is very important. Things need to take time. Repetition is a must, thanking everybody is a must. Patience is the key, and things need to take time. A Master of Ceremony (Toastmaster) keeps the paste and lead the protocol so to speak, while throwing out empty phrasing like they are candy; the big man, the man who changed the world, PHD from Harvard etc. "Give him another hand!" followed by a standing ovation, more buzzwords and bullshit. After about 1.5 hours of bullshit, it was now time for Lagerbäck to step up to the podium and lie, repeat himself and thank everybody for being there. While also repeating while everybody else said, to prove that he was actually paying attention, for at least an hour according to Nigerian customs.

He steps up, looks out into the huge crowd and says: "Let the feet do the talking" in classic Swenglish, and then steps down again.

The worst insult in Nigerian history. Not just a social faux pas as per the above mentioned customs. What Lagerbäck says can be translated into:

"Let's look at the facts", which is completely irrelevant from a Nigerian point of view. Nigerian soccer is all about nepotism, where players play because of kickback from the agents, not because of the skill of the players.

Talk about a cultural clash. You have to love the mix of the typical Swedish and the typical Nigerian.

I don't like soccer, but I will be cheering for the Nigerians. If for nothing else, for the nepotism. Lagerbäck should have read the part about conducting a Nigerian meeting that you can find towards the end of this book.

COWS ON THE RUNWAY

I found this status on Facebook, written by my buddy and Arik Air pilot Markus. Apparently, they couldn't land. The following exchange took place on Facebook:

Markus status: 30 minutes in holding due to "Cows on the Runway". I asked what they were doing there – got the answer that they are usually not there until around 1pm, but today they were a bit early. At least it's nice that the airport is considered part of the village.

Comment from one of Markus pilot friends: Haha! What airport? Port Harcourt? Didn't Air France bump into a couple of cows there? :)

Markus comment/reply: Benin actually. Associated were coming behind us and asked if they had given the cows "clear to land". The controller thought that we could land on the other runway since they were close to the threshold on rwy05, but what the hell, the runway isn't exactly long to begin with. It was better to wait for the poor farmers.

Markus elaborates further: It is relevant to inform you that there were about 200 cows there.

My comment: Outstanding.

HARMATTAN

Harmattan is a trade wind blowing all over Africa. All the sand and other debris makes it hard to see anything, or breathe for that matter. It's pretty much like if God blew a huge load all over Africa. You can find more academic approach on the matter elsewhere.

Since you can't see shit, the air traffic is hit by unreasonable delays. Add some Nigerian Donald Duck behavior and spice it up with frivolous airlines and mayhem follows as the natural fact. My good friend Petra had the pleasure to experience it.

Petra's name is in reality Peter and he works for Atlas Copco. He's a great guy and with his blond back-slick and preppy style he doesn't really look like he belongs here. He looks like a sheep ready for slaughter.

Petra was supposed to go ABUJA – LAGOS. Note that it's about 900 km, e.g. a 1 hour flight.

1. Petra was delayed 4 hours in Abuja.
2. Once in the air, the pilot went to the wrong airport. He went to Benin instead.
3. Furthermore, there are 2 Benin. One is a state in Nigeria, the other is the neighboring country Benin. Of course, he went to the neighboring country where they had to wait for 6 hours for the Harmattan wind to settle down. On top of that, they could not leave the airplane, because of visa-purposes (nobody wants 600 angry Nigerians in an airport). So they waited in the airplane, with the air condition turned off. It's far cry from a night on the Orient Express. Smell wise.
4. They landed in Lagos 13 hours later.
5. It would've taken 9 hours to go by car.

Fantastic!

THE LEANING TOWER OF PISA

What does this have to do with the 419's you might ask? You will soon find out.

One of our employees has a painting of the Leaning Tower of Pisa. It was hanging a bit askew, and his wife was trying to get this point across to the janitor working there. No wahala means no problem in Pidgin.

Day 1: Can you fix the painting, it's hanging askew.
Janitor: Yes Mam, No wahala
Day 2: Can you fix the painting, it's hanging askew.
Janitor: Yes Mam, No wahala
Day 3: Can you fix the painting, it's hanging askew.
Janitor: Yes Mam, No wahala
Day 4: Can you fix the painting, it's hanging askew.
Janitor: Yes Mam, No wahala

On the fifth day the wife lost her mind, asking the janitor in an angry tone when he's going to fix it.

The janitor got mad and expressed his confusion about the leaning tower. "Am I supposed to fix the tower or the painting!?"

Once again: Nigeria is the coolest country in the world.

ROLLING OVER A STEAM ROLLER – A DAY IN EQUATORILA GUINEA

We have a company located in EG, as we call it. It is a front for money laundering disguised as a construction company.

The locals there have limited knowledge (to be politically correct and to put it mildly). We have to recruit foreign personnel in order to execute manual casual labour. We're talking about truck drivers, crane operators etc.

To say the least, it is worrying that the human capital of a country gets shafted by Nigerian know-how. You got that right; we are hiring labourers from Nigeria that are considered cream of the crop here in EG.

Anyway, our DOO in EG, Becherra, gets a call – a local has managed to roll over a steam roller. Of course, this sounds like a made up story, an urban legend, so he makes his way to the site to check out if it really happened. And it did. No one knows how the hell the idiot managed to roll it over. It goes against all laws of physics. The steam roller reaches 3 km/h at maximum speed, it's insanely wide, long and weighs a ton. Bechara is no newbie to Africa, he is used to things not going according to plan, and does not chock easily. So, he arranges for a crane, gets the steam roller rolling again and everyone's happy.

Back at HQ after lunch, Bechera gets a call from Gulliermo informing him that the steam roller is on its back. Bechera says that he knows that, and that they fixed it. Gulliermo replies that no, that was this morning. He has managed to roll over the damn thing again.

TIA.

GOING TO THE HOSPITAL

Today, we will talk about hospitals. One of our employees purchased local ear swabs – a big mistake.

The cotton thingy gets stuck in the ear, I've experienced it myself, but since I'm metro sexual, I own a pair of tweezers.

The guy had to go to the hospital. He got the luxury treatment, walking past the dying people in the hallway. A local doctor sat him down and said, no problem, I can fix this, I just have to get the right tool, how about this one.

Yes, he used a plyer.

EGYPT AIR

The Egyptians landed here in Abuja and were about to unload the cargo. Probably it's like on Arik, meaning that eight people are standing still, smoking by the wing; the luggage will never arrive and they will blame it on being understaffed.

To speed up the process, an energetic Nigerian takes the matter into his own hands and gets a forklift. Very good very good. In the middle of the forking and unloading, he decided to leave the forklift with the forks in the same height as the plane, without pulling the handbrake.

The forklift rolls forward and boom, two fresh holes in the airplane body. What to do? This guy is definitely solution oriented, runs away and comes back with a welding tool.

The captain has at this stage had enough. He punches the guy so hard that he becomes part of the scenery.

COWBOY

You never cease to admire Nigerian ingenuity.

I've talked about their imaginative names, like for example the biggest crook in Nigeria appropriately named "Government" as his first name. I would like to be called that. Government Sabbagh.

Yesterday, in Lagos, we stumbled by a stroke of luck into a guy with the name:

COWBOY!

I remain,

Government Sabbagh

BILATERAL NEGOTIATIONS REGARDING NUCLEAR POWER

Hell might have frozen over. According to the phenomenal newspaper "This Day", you could read about how Nigeria and Iran has begun bilateral negotiations regarding nuclear power.

They also took the time to ensure the world that they want to extract uranium, solely for peaceful purposes, and that Iran seems like a very good collaborator.

On the question what the nuclear power was going to be used for, the answer was of course:

Energy and medicine.

The energy part I can understand even though I can't accept it. After all, it is a scary thought that Nigerians are going to be running a nuclear plant. As a foot note, there is actually a Nigerian space program and it managed to launch a satellite. Which they lost after 6 months in orbit. The following explanation was given to the press:

"Dat tin don vanisho. It don't scatta fo somewhere".

Meaning, it has vanished, and is scattered to God knows where.

What I don't understand is the other part, about using nuclear power for medical purposes. How does that work?

BUYING FRUIT AND VEGETABLES

The importance of clear instructions can never be underestimated in Nigeria.

One of our guys said to his maid:

-Buy kiwi and avocado

She came back with an avocado and kiwi shoe polish. (In her defense though, kiwi is not part of the local fauna, or as an imported product).

Drum roll.

PIZZA FOR LUNCH

In Asokor hotel:

(Lunch break at work):

1. Arrive at 12pm.
2. Get seated next to the stork (there's an actual stork there).
3. Order lunch, preferably a four season pizza with beef, tomato, cheese, mushrooms and so on.
4. Drink beer until 3pm, because you're hungry and the food hasn't arrived yet.
5. At 3pm the food arrives, the pizza consists of tuna and canned white beans.
6. Eat anyway because you are drunk and starving.
7. Go to the car and drive back to the office.
8. Get stuck in traffic.
9. Be back at work at about 5.30pm.

Government Sabbagh.

OUR LIST OF DICTATORS

In the absence of things to do, we have made a list of dictators of the century, where, not unsuspectingly despite its many democracies, Africa is heavily overrepresented.

Some people might think that Stalin or Hitler should make the list, but in our opinion, you have to be able to hand over the power, a transition. That is the most important criteria. To rule after you are dead. Just being a mass murdering asshole is not enough.

The criteria and the list are as follow:

Criteria:
- A long time in power, and a semi-peaceful reign. At least a decade.
- A successful transition within the family (extended family included), preferably non-violent.
- At least 10% of the country's population executed, or squashed/imprisoned/tortured in one way or another.
- Having waged war against minorities in the country.
- Engaged in border disputes with unrealistic demands. (We are ready to negotiate about the Golan-heights, but we want India in return).
- Individual concoction of ideology.
- Personality cult. (Kim Jong Il played golf 15 times, and have made 76 hole in ones).
- Apartment in Paris, London, New York or any other expensive high profile city. Lavishly decorated and funded with the tax payers money. A good example is the Sultan of Brunei's residence in LA, fully staffed, which he has never visited.
- A developed ability in giving the Security Council a headache (never-ending discussions, veto blocking). Much like Kaddafi's one hour speech in Arabic in front of the Security Council way over his allocated ten minutes. A speech that had no political point what so ever.
- Associated with an animal. Hafez el Assad, who was associated with a lion, an association he nurtured himself. Because of his last name which means lion in Arabic.
- Native wife from the upper-class and at the same time screwing blond models. This goes without saying. "Power is sexy" to quote Henry Kissinger.
- Owning or at least supporting a team in the national sport.
- Claiming ownership of a bizarre scientific discovery. "I invented H2O", or even better, claiming you can cure AIDS with bananas like Gambian President Yahya Jammeh.

The list so far:

- Kim Il Sung succeeded by Kim Jong Il, who is succeeded by Kim Jong Un. This is unheard of in modern times. A three-generation rule, according to our criteria. You can go as far as calling it a dictator hat trick, if Kim Jong Un manages a successful transition. It is only dwarfed by the three-generation rule of Swaziland, which contains one female ruler.
- Papa Doc succeeded by his more boyish son with the name Baby Doc.
- Hafez el Assad succeeded by his son, the dentist/dictator Bashar el Assad.
- Labotsibeni Gwamile Mdluli, the only matriarch on the list, ruled Swaziland between 1899-1921 before she handed over power to her son Sobhuza II. Sobhuza II in turn had a big talent pool to choose from when it came to his successor. He had 70 wives, 210 children and 1000 grandchildren. Luckily he found a man who could rule, and he was succeeded by Mswati III one of his sons, who in many ways is a player in his own right. He gathers the country's most beautiful virgins under the age of 18 on a yearly basis and deflowers them royally, and then marries the one who gets knocked up. He is suspected to have contracted HIV, which, with his highly polygamous lifestyle makes him the single most traceable HIV spreading source in the world. If that is not enough, Swaziland is from a Gini index point of view one of the worst countries in the world. Gini index stretches from 0-100, where 0 is perfect equality, which means that every person in the said country owns as much as the other. 100 is perfect inequality which means that one person owns all assets in a country while the rest of the population owns absolutely nothing. The index for Sweden is 27,3, which should work as a bench mark. Depending on how you frame the question, Swaziland's Gini index is between 51,5-70 (the figures are difficult to trust as they are not the most transparent country in the world). This basically translates to Mswati III owning two thirds of the countries assets.
- King Hussein of Jordan, the least eccentric on the list, but however worthy of being here. Handed over power to his son King Abdallah II, who continues in the same bravado manner as his father, by flying strike air plane missions and engaging in warfare, while flipping of Palestinians.

- Gnassingbé Eyadéma, the president of Togo, was at the time of his death, Africa's number one ruler with 38 years in power. He seized power according to the African tradition, by a coup d'état. He was reelected 72, 79, 86, 93, 98 and 03 with no political opposition what so ever. He died in a heart attack in 2005 but, had thank God changed the constitution just days before so his son could succeed him. And rightly so, he was succeeded by his son Faure Gnassingbé, who seems to harness the same disdain for his people as his father.

People who will make the list as soon as they can arrange for a transition*:
- Teodore Obiang (gets extra points for first helping his uncle, the ruler at the time, to slaughter his own family, then overthrows him and executes him with a firing squad because of his atrocities against the same family).
- Paul Biya
- Nguesso Sassou
- Hosni Mubarak
- Muammar Khadaffi
- Stroessner

*This list was composed before the Arabic spring, which further more proves the point, that the transition is the most important criteria. And the most difficult one. Khaddafi is dead, so is Stroessner. Mubarrak is imprisoned. However Paul Biya of Cameroun, Obiang of Equatorial Guinea still are very much in the game. Congo's Sassou is on the list, because he has managed to fulfill all criteria's except the transition, however the possibility of him shifting power to a family member is measly to say the least. Once again we end with a Prince Philip quote, upon his state visit to Stroessners Paraguay he said: "It's a pleasure to be in a country that isn't ruled by its people."

Government Sabbagh.

GIVING ILLEGAL TIPS

In Nigeria, you can give illegal tips. At performances, live music, dance or any other kind of circus act, it's customary to walk up to the performers with a bundle of money and, so to speak, make it rain, or press the money onto the sweaty forehead of the artist. It's a sign of generosity and good taste. Some people might find it vulgar and disparaging. Luckily, it's illegal because it's an insult to:
MONEY!
Not against the guy that gets money attached to his forehead. Once again I ask myself; who's thinking, how are they thinking and what the hell are they thinking?

MY FATHA DON DIE

Hussein is a cool dude that works for us. He is Lebanese man, born and raised here and he, if anyone, knows the culture and the people. He is fluent in Pidgin, Hausa, Igbo and Yoruba. He knows the ropes.
The following exchange took place:

Local Employee: "Masta (Master), my father don die, I need to go village", i.e. his father has died and he needs to go to the village.
Hussein: No problem —Hussein gives him some money, the guy leaves and after a while, comes back.
One week later,
Local Employee: "Masta my father don die, I need to go village".

Hussein gives him some money; the guy leaves and after a while, comes back.
He keeps doing this a couple of times. A couple of times too many in our opinion. Hussein falls for it again and again, and this makes us question his sanity, and the notion that Hussein for some reason has no clue of what he is doing anymore starts to take on a life of its own. Upon confronting him, He just shrugs, dismisses you, and basically just ignores you.
Not to anyone's surprise, the same topic of conversation happened again, but this time with a new twist:

Local Employee: "Masta, my motha don die, I need to go to village".

Hussein kindly agrees and helps him out, and the company is in a state of chock. No one understands Hussein's reasoning.

Another two weeks pass, and the same thing happens again.

Local Employee: "My motha don die" etc.

This time though, Hussein loses it completely, he spits in his hand, and then slaps a guy. (The spitting part is very Middle Eastern, it is done to increase the sound upon slapping someone, and increase pain, but also keep nosy people away).

"It's one thing if you don't know who screwed your mother, but you can only exit out of one vagina!"
Nice huh? Most of us would have lost it when he claimed his father died twice, but it would be a rookie-mistake to think that monogamy exists in Africa. Thanks Hussein, for teaching us a very important lesson.

SMALL ACCIDENT

I am sitting in my office, minding my own business, drinking pot after pot of Arabic/Turkish coffee, and smoking as much as my lungs can muster, while being as colonial as humanly or inhumanly possible. A regular day at work, in other words.

A crane operator walks into my office, and the following dialog unfolds:

Local: SAAAAAAAAAA! (Sir)
Me: Abi na wettin? (What is it?)
Local: Oga, a dey make small accident (Sir, I have had a small accident).
Me: No wahala, make we go see'am. (No problem, let us go inspect it).
As we walk out, I see that the crane has run over 5 brand new pick-up trucks. My blood pressure rises and my voice spirals out of control.
Me: Wettin you dey do? Dis na be small accident? Wettin de happon? You de craze etc. (What did you do? Is this a small accident? What happened? Are you crazy?)
Local: Oga sorryo (Please pardon me Sir).
Me: It's like Nicolas Cage said in "Lord of War", in moments of extreme anger or ecstasy you revert to your mother tongue.

HRH

I've told you about our king Chief Ukwu. I feel like it's time for an update on him. The thing with all kings in Nigeria is that they have their own registration plates, and I don't mean some nifty vanity plate. They get their title and a number, so HRH (His Royal Highness) 123 for example. Additionally he gets a crown, or more accurately a baseball cap with HRH sown onto it a bit willy-nilly.

Queen Elizabeth, there is something here for you to learn.

SPELLING IN PIDGIN

Spelling in Pidgin can look like this:

L for elephant

A for education (aducashion)

G for Jesus

O for nothing

S for etc.

The letters follow the pronunciation. Btw, the O for nothing comes from them using an o as filler at the end of the word; it doesn't have any real meaning. Anyway, we just spelled LAGOS. For anyone not keeping up, the spelling has nothing to do with the first letter in the word, but with the pronunciation. I can inform you that it takes some time getting used to.

UGELLI

Yesterday, my colleague came back from Ugelli, with tinted car windows. To me, this is completely insane since the electricity here is non-existing, especially street lighting. Add to that the fact that people are walking out into the street all the time and we can agree that it's not the best of ideas.

But in Ugelli you apparently need to have tinted windows if you're white, otherwise you get kidnapped in a flash.

WHEN SOFIE PURCHASED SUNSCREEN

The first time Sofie arrived in Nigeria, she didn't bring sunscreen, so her first order of business was to go to the local supermarket to buy some. Sofie kindly approached the clerk to ask if they had sunscreen. The clerk looked at Sofie like she was from the moon, and then walked away. Of course, I interjected and took control of the situation.

But why does our beloved Nigerian react like this? The following reasoning took place her brain:

1. Sunscreen, what's that?
2. Why does she want to sit in the sun? What is wrong with these crazy white people?

It goes without a saying that the Nigerians don't use sunscreen and that they avoid the sun as much as possible, and of course, they have no understanding for the fact that anyone wants to sit in the sun. Again, culture clash.

IS NIGERIA REALLY A THIRD WORLD COUNTRY?

It's time again for another 419. Today, we are going to compare Nigeria with England. For some reason, England is said to be a developed country. I will now bust that myth based on my last visit.

Transportation
England: In the city of London you can walk or grab a cab if you're in a hurry. I spent the hefty sum of £700 in one week.

Nigeria: For £1000 you have paid your driver's entire annual salary.

Shopping
England: Pretty bland, you can buy everything.

Nigeria: The supply is so bad that you have to get creative, which is invigorating.

Household services
England: Tough shit when you have to iron your own shirt and even worse when you have to turn your underwear inside-out.

Nigeria: The maid runs the household. The clothes are washed every day.

Coffee in the office
England: No coffee girls, you got to get your own coffee. Embarrassing when you have a visitor.

Nigeria: Chichi brings coffee every time you call on her.

Airport
England: Stand politely in every damn line.

Nigeria:
Harry our airport protocol officer handles the check in the prior day and hangs onto our passports. We walk straight to the gate without passing security five minutes before departure.

Electricity
England: An excessive amount of electricity all day.

Nigeria: No, little or extremely expensive around the clock electricity powered by diesel generators puts you on your toes.

Taxes
England: Shamelessly high taxes.

Nigeria: Shamelessly high bribes.

Humanity
England: Everyone is equal.

Nigeria: Your value as a human being is strongly related to your net worth.

Conclusion: England is a third world country.

DEFINING INFLATION

A guy, we can call him X, was present at a meeting at CBN, i.e. Central Bank of Nigeria, where they were trying to determine the monetary inflation, and what they were thinking it would be. Members from ECOWAS, the EU Commission and bureaucrats from the embassies were also present, at least I think they were, if they weren't it makes the story even better. Person Y arise and puts on a PowerPoint presentation filled with facts regarding what he thought the inflation should be, devaluations that could affect it, the situation in the delta, the oil; he did a great job with some solid research.

At this point you should've learned that this is a big mistake. Facts are not prime real estate in Nigeria, and this guy was probably a newbie. So, how did they handle the information and how did they use it to proceed in determining the pace of inflation?

They did the only right thing, in the spirit of flea market negotiation, they split into two camps where one camp started with 15%, the other thought 2% was more reasonable and so on. It went on for a couple of hours as they were trying to convince each other, and not unexpectedly it ended up in the middle, around 6%.

If you're a professor in economics you are probably about to faint.

THE ART OF EATING DOG

You see, eating dog is an art form; it's nothing you just do on a whim, grabbing the first dog you see on the street. It takes finesse, strategy and gastronomical knowledge. Now you might be thinking: how is that? Is there a difference between breads? Can I as a dog-person live in

Nigeria with my dog without fear of my dog getting eaten? The answer is yes, at least according to a friend's driver Charlie who told me: "Well, we eat dogs, but not expat dogs, you can't eat them because they are filled with vaccines, because white people are crazy, they take their dogs to the doctor, so we stay away from them."

There you have it.

GETTING KIDNAPPED, AN EXPERIENCE OR A TOTAL DISASTER?

A very controversial subject to say the least. The Nigerians are infamous for their kidnappings, and people are in general scared shitless about getting kidnapped. With that in mind, we're going to have a look at two situations and try something that could be thought of as a psychological analysis.

One of our guys got kidnapped six years ago, and it was obviously very dramatic. He went on a RIB boat for five hours past swamplands, into strange caverns in the south, it was cold, windy etc. I bet it was a horrible experience. But listen to this, this was his comment. We were sitting, talking about Colombia. They sure don't have the best reputation in the world either. Some things are probably better there than in Nigeria though, like the Colombian girls - their national pride. This guy says: "Oh my god, you can't go to Colombia, it's really dangerous there, and you can get kidnapped." So this guy lives in Nigeria, has gotten kidnapped once and thinks Colombia is dangerous. You have to wonder, how does his reasoning work?

The next cool kidnapping story revolves around one of our own guys. He broke the safety regulations and decided to let the police escort go ahead of him, allowing him to inspect the construction site and come 10 minutes late for lunch. IQ of a dirty sock. It took 7 minutes and he was gone, taken away to some dump in the bush.

But this is where the story starts. The kidnappers get in contact with one of our mediators and demands something along the line of £1.5 million. We tell them, on the spot, no. He didn't follow the safety protocol so we're not going to pay. They then ask (he is Lebanese) if the state can pay. No, we answer, look at him, he's 70 years old and still working, if we had a state that took responsibility, he would be home, retired and enjoying his pension. Oh, they said, but what about his family? Check the guys mouth, we said, half of his teeth are missing, his family has no money. The kidnappers are starting to get frustrated now. Just as they were about to hang up we made up a story about him having a disease and that they have to buy medicine worth the equivalent of two annual salaries for him or he will die.

The Nigerians are real business men so they understand the importance of keeping the guy alive in order to get paid. At the same time they understand when they don't have a paying customer. So, what do they do in order to minimize the risks and get out of a bad deal? They want us to cover the costs of getting him back, about £700.

Negotiation tactics at its finest.

FLYING BA TO NIGERIA

The BA flight between London and Nigeria might be one of the most profitable in the world. It's always crowded, and I mean really crowded, with like 600 people in one airplane. It's a bit interesting that this flight has never been affected by worker strikes, but the answer is probably simple; who wants 600 angry Nigerians in an airport in London? No one.

The entire phenomenon is very strange. It starts in Nigeria where the airplane is filled with people, but with very little hand luggage. First class, business class, premium economy and economy are crowded.

Additionally, you have to endure people talking on the phone even though we're in the air, people who think that they're supposed to be seated in 26B because that is the seat they've had before, no matter what their current ticket is saying. "Why did he get three meatballs when I only got 2" is another fun discussion you get to experience. "Put the entire bottle of wine here" is another thing you will hear, i.e., "give me the entire bottle so I can take it home".

One time, the guy seated next to me thought that the movie I was watching was bad, so he changed the movie, on my own personal screen.

When you go to London, it's a completely different story. It's like a swarm of grasshoppers roaming the airport, shopping everything that gets in their way. Everyone has at least four gigantic bags each, filled with frying pans, razors and everything else they can get hold of. At the gate, they give the call that it's time for boarding. They start with first class and business class. To the surprise of no one, everyone stands up and starts running into the airplane, no matter what their ticket says. And if you don't, you won't have room for your hand luggage.

Don't take my word for it though. I will quote a British woman, who works as a stewardess and speaks pidgin. She is quite the phenomenon and goes by the name Oyinbo Princess. Beware of pidgin in writing.

"One day a de take flight, go 9ija, na ma job inside di plain bi dat, so I de enta di plain, do my norma norma security check everytin. Everybody de enta, omo di flight don full die.(...) **Omo people de carry loado, no bi say anything, na di load who de carry, if you dey se am, you go fear self, how we go fittam inside di plain"**

When arriving to Nigeria, there is absolutely nothing left of the airplane.

NIGERIA-NORTH KOREA

Like most people, I assume you have followed the world cup of soccer with great excitement. I haven't, because soccer doesn't interest me in the slightest. Once again, 22 nut-jobs chasing a piece of plastic on a grass field might just be the most insane timewaster there is. Add to that grown men yelling at each other, thumping their chests – it's just not for me. Well, yelling and thumping my chest might be my thing, but it will definitely not be soccer that provokes these feelings in me.

I did however watch Nigeria – North Korea. It was a fun watch. The North Koreans were psychologically beaten before they even entered the field. The reason was not that they knew that Kimmy (Kim Jong) was going to beat the crap out of them if they lost, but that the difference in penis size never have been greater than during this game.

YELLOW FEVER

When Sofie was coming to visit the first time, it was a bit difficult to arrange for the vaccinations. She was living in Berlin, so I had to organize it all from Nigeria, i.e. filling in the VISA application, trying to figure out her eye colour etc. It wasn't easy, but I managed. The problem was finding a place in Berlin where she could get a vaccination for the yellow fever. I'm not at a premium with her father (still not), and sneaking her to Nigeria behind his back and sending her back with malaria and yellow fever would probably not be a hit. Her dad would have shot me upon landing at Arlanda. So I tried to find a clinic that would give her the vaccine. Of course, it didn't go well. Communicating with the Germans didn't go well, trying to pay went even worse and I don't even think we were talking about the same medicines. So I did the only right thing, I went down to Dr. Hassan's clinic in Wuse 2 and said the following:

>Me: Dr. Hassan, how are you?
>Dr. Hassan: Perpetual pain, how are you?
>Me: I'm brilliant. Hey, I have a problem that you might be able to solve.
>Dr. Hassan: And what might that be?
>Me: The thing is, my woman is on her way down here and I can't "find" any time for a yellow fever vaccination. She's coming in a month, and you know how fussy they are concerning vaccines in Europe and all that.
>Dr. Hassan: I see, you want me to give you a yellow card dated in the future, even though she hasn't received the vaccine and never been to Nigeria before, issued by the Ministry of Health?
>Me: Pretty much, yes.
>Dr. Hassan: When is she coming?
>Me: Seventh of November.
>Dr. Hassan: Alright, I'll write the seventh then, is that fine?
>Me: Perfect.

Totally free from complications and bureaucracy. You just have to love this banana republic, right?

I racked up everything, sent the papers to Germany and just like that, we're vaccinated and done.

MY DRIVERS

I could write an entire book about this subject. My first driver's name was Patrick, a guy in his 30's from Rivers, which is a really cool state that specializes in graduating criminals and also happens to be where I had my first encounter with Nigeria's version of Human Resources.

I decided to get really serious, giving him an in detail job description consisting of 30 pages regulating his entire day up to the smallest detail. There were no question marks regarding what he was going to do, how he was going to do it and when it was going to be done. I was running this guy's life for two months with great results. Of course, everyone was laughing at me in the beginning, thinking it was a waste of time, but as time went I could brag about how reliable and loyal my driver was. I had minimized all risks of theft, fraud and other fraudulent activities. I was incredibly pleased and proud of what I had achieved.

Apparently, that was wrong. The guy had a need to ventilate these feelings somewhere. If I remember correctly, it was a Tuesday at 7pm when I was exiting HQ to go home. I was pretty surprised to not find Patrik anywhere, he had disappeared without a trace and his phone was shut off.

When I got home, I called the police and informed them about the situation, and I had to wait patiently until the next morning to get any information. Apparently, Patrick had snitched the car, picked up a buddy, armed themselves to the teeth, stopped two cars and robbed them of everything they owned, got chased by the cops and then wrecked the car into a wall. Of course, I had to pay something like £2500 to the cops, to compensate for something I don't know, I just wanted my car.

THE 419'S - a travelogue about a country on crack

The following day, I get a call from Patrick, asking for my forgiveness and explaining to me that he had to do it as he needed the money. He also asked if he could come to work. You have to give him credit for being brave.

I changed driver to Sam.

Sam was 50 years old and drove like a bat out of hell. He wrecked the car like 3 times in 2 months. Additionally, his hearing was like that of a 100 year old. I got the feeling that he was kind, but a few cans short of a six pack.

I ditched my organized approach and started giving orders using text messages. After 4 weeks of orders through text messages that he never seemed to follow, I went completely mad and yelled at him until my blood started boiling. Turns out that he couldn't read or write. You'd think that someone would inform me of that earlier, or that I would figure it out myself, but nope.

The straw that broke the camel's back happened a lovely morning when I went to the dentist to fix two of my teeth without anesthesia. I went back to the office and made an attempt to sit on my chair, which decided to roll back making me fall on my ass.

I had had enough, so I decided to go home. Arriving at my house, Sam decided to mash my fingers between the window and the door, and in the middle of all the yelling as I had my fingers stuck he does the following instead of rolling down the damn window:

Oga, Sorry, Oga A Beg I am sorry etc.

My fingers are still stuck as he is telling me this, and I'm trying to make him understand that his excuses are redundant as long as he opens the window!

At last, I got my fingers out, and he got fired. I went home to lick my wounds.

The next guy was Akin. He was extremely unreliable and unpleasant.

Not that he did anything in particular, but he had a sleazy feeling to him. At this point in time, I had started to amass quite a bit of knowledge, I was getting to know the ropes.

Akin made no mistakes up until recently. He was going to pick me up at the airport. He goes there on the wrong day, drunk and wrecks the car.

The lesson learned, is, that if I think a driver should be hired, he is most probably useless.

PAPA TOUFIC IS GOING TO BUY CIGARETTES

In terms of character, there is no one like Toufic. Let's start with a quick introduction of the man in question. He is 73 years old, he is slower than a sloth in terms of pace. He has a comb over that puts Danny Devito to shame, smokes 5 packs of gauloises a day, and has mastered the craft to always have a cigarette in his mouth and talk at the same time, without the ash leaving the cigarette. His hair, mustache and fingers have turned into that nice, tea-yellow color. The kind of color that could make you think that he has been dipped in Lipton. He smokes so much that his secretary demanded a "cancer allowance" as a surcharge on her salary to atone for the torture that she had to live with, in spite of her making the active choice not to smoke.

Since he's as old as the hills, he goes by the nickname Papa Toufic, or simply Papa. The thing is that Papa is unexpectedly competent, while still being extremely slow due to his old age; a story will start about 2000 years B.C and he has a tendency to enter all discussions with a know-it-all attitude out of this world. You feel like a three year old when talking to him.

This time, Papa was in Nigeria, making his way into the outskirts to show his displeasure and in general leaving a lead-heavy cloud of anxiety over the entire project. I think it was in Ondo, but that is of less significance. From the airport, it takes four hours to make your way to the site, located out in the bush.
In the car, Papa is surprising no one as he is tearing the project manager apart to get him into the right frame of mind, detailing all the errors he has committed in this project, in the last project, all the errors he will

make and remind everyone about all his shortcomings, reducing him to becoming a shell of a man. When Papa is in the middle of this sadistic momentum he has a tendency to completely forget his surroundings, lighting cigarette after cigarette and piles on until this guy feels like crap and on the edge of despair with strong contemplations of committing suicide.

Like they say, karma is a bitch. Just as Papa is about to deliver the killing blow, he discovers that he only has two cigarettes left, resulting in a panic attack. The last comment regarding how much the project manager sucks doesn't materialize, and thus, God has saved another life. Now, the problem starts revolving around if Papa can survive with only two cigarettes. He starts writhing in cold sweat, loses his ability to speak but quickly remains his composure, grabs one of the cigarettes and shows it to the driver:
"Go buy one like this".

The driver says "sure" and everyone gets out of the car. He puts the pedal to the metal and drives towards civilization. A four hour trip, one way, I might add.

At the compound, Papa is sitting in the dining room acting grumpy, trying to survive the worst eight hours of his life, which for everyone else mean eight hours of rest, eight hours without anxiety.
8 hours later, the driver finally returns with a big smile on his lips, runs towards Papa and gives him ONE CIGARETTE!

Papa takes it, puts it in his pack and goes to sleep. He goes back to Abuja the day after.
God is good. The project leader didn't take his own life this time either.

NEWSPAPER ALLOWANCE

Should you become a minister in Nigeria or in England? The answer is pretty simple. European politicians work for the people, or on behalf of. Maybe you feel like you are being misrepresented, and all politicians are a-holes. But as life goes, it's all about perspective, and everything is relative.

It's a completely different story in Nigeria. If you aren't exploiting the people, you aren't cut out to be a politician. Apart from the mile high minister salaries, they get an annual allowance of about £150,000. This allowance is for newspapers. In other words, you get an annual allowance just to be able to shop for reading material, in order to keep up with the world. There's of course no need to show the receipts, they are trusted to spend this money on newspapers and other reading material.

It doesn't take a whole lot of mental arithmetic to come to the conclusion that we're talking about £300 a day to buy magazines. That means 300 newspapers a day, if you're only reading news, and maybe 200 newspapers a day if you throw in some porn magazines, some car magazines etc. To put in in perspective for you. The American president gets an annual amount of $50,000 non-taxable expense allowance to assist in defraying expenses. An amount that has not been revised since 2001.

SOLVING THE AIDS CRISIS

There's a lot of talk about Aids in Africa. Well, not in Africa, but when the west talks about Africa. They talk about limiting the proliferation of HIV, educating people in sex and all kinds of western empty phrases to make them look like good Samaritans. Of course, I see straight past the academic corps, doctors without borders and other idiot organizations that claims that so and so many die from Aids every year. The fact is that they die well before they die of Aids. In Nigeria, or in Africa in general, you either die in traffic or from malaria, no matter if you have HIV or not, and that's where you need to focus your efforts. Anyway, this is not meant to be a serious NGO-report so let's change the tone immediately. Let's start with malaria, a deadly disease if it isn't treated – you die from high fever. This is not really an issue for people that can afford health care. I treat my malaria quarterly, and it's as exciting every time. There's a bunch of symptoms you get from the medicine. Of course, I get them all within 15 minutes of one and other for three days. The two I don't get are blindness and red rashes. The side effects are the following, alternating for three days:

THE 419'S-a travelogue about a country on crack

1. Horny as a teenager for about 15 minutes.
2. Depression, 15 minutes.
3. Hallucinations, 15 minutes.
4. Indescribable joy, 15 minutes.
5. Fibrillation, 15 minutes.
6. Uncontrollable crying (nobody likes me), 15 minutes.

It goes without saying that you are kind of beaten down and emotionally shaken after three days of this. You also need another three days of rest in order to not start crying at an important meeting or feeling the need to mount the car when you're at your horniest.

This was a parenthesis. Getting back to the gay plague, or HIV and Aids as it's called in more academic terms. I have a good friend who works for a charity organization, and this organization is apparently as tired as all the other non-profit organizations.

Their mission was to not only reach out to people on the streets and inform them about the gay plague, but also to hand out free condoms, meant to be used in conjunction with intercourse and other non-Christian behavior.

They let the locals prepare everything, including condoms and flyers, and my good friend that at the time had zero experience of Nigeria left them to handle the preparations alone. When they were ready, they went out into the field to inform and spread the message with flyers and condoms.

The thing is, Nigerians are really damn efficient. They never do more than they have to, and some rising star came up with the idea that it would be stupid to spend energy in both handing out a flyer and a condom and decided to mix the two into one action. A good thought. So when my good friend goes out into the field to check up on them, she sees the result and immediately starts pulling her own hair. They have stapled the condoms onto the flyers, and to make matters worse, already handed most of them out.

She came running to me, crying, hysterical and in panic. She expected some kind of support. My answer:

Welcome to Nigeria.

"NIGAS"

This is totally amazing, even for me. The thing is, dear friends, readers and everyone else that some Nigerian authority has decided to start a joint venture with Gazprom. Gazprom is a Russian gas company owned by old communist bigwigs and all kinds of crooks. The Chairman was elected by Putin and just so happens to be the minister of energy. A company well suited for Nigeria by the looks of it.

In some weird way Gazprom and some other Nigerian authority found each other and start negotiation a joint venture designated to extract gas. The thing is, Gazprom will not do this themselves, but in collaboration with some Donald Duck authority, or with the government, or the state as co-owner.

Anyway, they manage to find an agreement in this potpourri of communists and capitalists and people are flown across the world to be able to participate at the round table in Nigeria.

Old men from Russia dressed in funny suits are now sitting at the same table as big boned Nigerians in dresses and silly hats, ready to negotiate. They talk about what the ownership structure should look like, what kind of governance framework they should use, who will be members of the board, candidates for Chairman, business plans, volumes to extract, where and how they are to be sold, to what price, what to do if the world market price drops, how much needs to be invested into building facilities, should we fly down Putin so that he can eat dog and drink vodka with Yar Adua?

How can we solve the security problem? How can we make sure they don't start blowing up the pipelines? How can we handle the locals when we're constructing the gas pipelines?

As you can see, it's not a simple project – a lot of things to consider.

THE 419´S-a travelogue about a country on crack

They manage to handle all of this with flying colours, they actually manage to agree on everything. Despite the cultural difference and all of what that entails. Business without borders is born.

What's even more astonishing is what they manage to agree on next. The name. "We're naming ourselves the Nigerian Gas Association!" Everyone nods, hums and are pleased about their joint venture name. The thing is, in Nigeria, you don't get by without an abbreviation. So, one of these nutjobs says the following:

"Nigas" will be our abbreviation. The jubilation and applause knew no bounds. The day after you can hear the following when you call the "Nigas" switch board.

"Nigas", how can I help you? It very much sounds like "Niggers, how can I help you?"

Of course, I called several times and laughed more and more every time.

SAFA´S BROTHEL IN LAGOS

Everyone that has been keeping up with the terminology understands the terms antelopes and gazelles, but the thing is, not every John likes the local talent. That's where Safa, a Moroccan madam with her base in Lagos, enters the frame. One guy, we can call him X, had been in Abuja for about three weeks and had one week left before he was going to leave the place.

During these three weeks, he had gone through some of the local talent but he got tired of it and started to, well, go for whiter hookers.

Since the large expat community is located in Lagos, he came to the brilliant conclusion to start looking there. He googled, checked networks (researching internet forums, talked to the guys and rooted around for Intel) and came to the conclusion that if you want white chicks, you talk to Safa. Safa's is from Morocco and I've unfortunately never had the honor to meet her, but the image of an Arabic madam, is terrifying. I'm imagining a hog beast-like crone with a moustache that puts mine to shame and body hair that make me look like a newborn infant. Add to that gigantic biceps that make any man or woman shit themselves, hands to remind everyone that she has worked for 10 years in the mines before she started her new "business", her being dwarf-like in height, and a situation where the back of her knees make contact with her ass cheeks

Anyway, X miraculously gets her phone number, calls her up and she dishes out the conditions. You have to pay the round-trip to Lagos, are you ok with that? Yes, he says. You have to pick her up at the airport, are you ok with that? Yes, he says. You have to pay upfront, are you ok with that? Yes, he says.

After they have sorted out the "terms and conditions", X decides to ask a question to make sure that the goods are of quality.

"Safa, are the girls white?"

No, she answers sarcastically, I import Negros to Nigeria, and hung up the phone.

Safa 1 point, X 0 points.

PRICE WATERHOUSE COOPERS VISITS CLUB MED NIGERIA

As it turns out, one of the companies in our group had one of the worst finance departments on earth. Getting an income statement and balance report up to date was seemingly impossible. To illustrate how far behind they were, you had to settle for a report that was three months old. This lead to that all financial decisions were made on a whim and you never had a damn clue where you stood economically. This might fly if you're a pizzeria parlor in Leeds, but we're talking about a 450 multi-million pound business here.

Of course, this is a disaster, so they decided to bring in PWC and their phenomenal, dolled up services. The project manager was scared to

THE 419'S-a travelogue about a country on crack

death to go to Nigeria. He googled, gathered information, listened to what people had to say, and the more he found out, the less he wanted to go. Nigeria doesn't have the best reputation in the world, and the more you dig, the worse it gets.

Add to that that the guy was scared of flying and got the information that there are no radars in Nigeria; the pilots are using the front window to see if there are any other airplanes nearby. He has become religious after flying, after having squeezed the arm rest on the airplane to pieces. Not to anyone's surprise, he was an emotional wreck when he landed. And that's OK, as long as you don't land in Lagos International Airport. If Jesus had landed in Lagos International Airport he would have crucified himself before going through customs. It's a horrible airport. Everything is chaos, everyone is getting paid, everything you do is wrong, you're standing in the wrong line, you have the wrong name, you're wanted by the police, you have the wrong clothes, your VISA is a counterfeit – everything you can imagine. Let's not even talk about the business lounge. It costs 10 pounds to enter, so it has nothing to do with flying business class or not, and you can smoke in there so everyone is cramped into that spot and the rest of the airport is empty. We can establish that it smells nothing like roses in there.

Of course, all of this makes the project manager extra nervous; no one wants to go to jail in Nigeria, and he starts doubting his own VISA, his clothes, if he's standing in the right line etc.

Anyway, he miraculously passes the passport control and is met by the next Olympic sport, trying to get hold of your luggage. Now you have to try to understand how this guy is feeling. First, he thinks he's going to die on the plane. When he has survived that adventure he thinks he is going to end up in a Nigerian prison. Simply put, this is not the time and place to give this guy a scare, not even as a joke.

So he's standing there next to the conveyor belt, shitting bricks and just wants to get out of there as soon as possible. Suddenly, a thunderous sound is heard from above. The inner roof is rumbling down and a giant snake lands just next to where he is standing. The project manager gets his third heart attack. We, on the other hand, get a new story.

THE EMIR OF BIDA OFFERS TURNKEY SOLUTIONS

Before talking about what kind of solution the Emir has offered us, I want to talk a little bit about Bida and the Emirate. The Emirate is located in Nigeria and is a Kingdom with the Emir as a ruler, in a republic. I have no damn idea how they make sense of that and how it works, and I'm guessing no one else does either so there is no reason to ask. It's just the way it is.

One of many tribes in Nigeria, the tribe of Nupe, is located in the Emirate. Just like people in the U.K have a national insurance number, you have something similar in Bida – you make three cuts on each side of the cheeks making it look like a cat moustache in order to define what tribe you belong to and that will be your look for the rest of your life.

There are more modern elements of the Emirate (it should be added that they are Muslims), for example the zero tolerance policy against bigamy. Alhaji Muhammadu Bello Masaba is born Nupe and part of the Emirate. Unlike many other men, he thought that women are easy to handle and thus decided to get married. With 86 women, more particularly. He managed to stay married to them for a long time, until people found out. Housing 86 women with children normally won't go unnoticed, or when you buy them all tampons as they are synchronizing their monthlies, or the share amount of family feuds that must have been going on – you can't miss that. Someone managed to notice this thing that everyone else had missed and called the cops. The Emir was in chock, he had no clue, he hadn't seen or heard anything - it had passed him by completely. He gave his thanks to the police for this phenomenal discovery and threatened the man in question with the death penalty if he didn't immediately divorce 82 of the 86 wives. After all, you don't have to go overboard with things. Four wives will have to do. The Emir once again became an enlightened despot and was celebrated by the entire country.

Another modern element is the annual festival where they celebrate the greatness of the Emir. They do this with a huge parade consisting of a couple of hundred horses. Incredibly cool, but animal lovers would probably faint as they used barbed wire and razor blades on a metal piece in the horses' mouths instead of regular bit shanks.

The thing is, this parade of horses is pretty labour intensive. They don't just ride the horses; they have to care for them during the entire year. The Emir solved this problem 300 years ago and it still holds as a great, modern solution. They have simply enslaved part of their own tribe, which works for the Kingdom with all kinds of tasks, where working with the horses is one of the most prestigious. Luckily, they have also solved recruiting; your children belong to the kingdom and are born into slavery in order to inherit their parents' tasks. This is the year 2010, I might add.

The Germans own a stable and we wanted to buy a horse. As they aren't better than the Lebanese, we always try to one-up each other until the brink of ruin in the true spirit of napoleon complexes. I always say that the Lebanese are the only people that borrow money in order to buy something they can't afford, don't need and only want in order to impress someone they don't like. So we started to look around and we were thinking about buying a horse from Kano. It just so happens that the Emir is a good friend of ours. He found out about this through the jungle telegrams and became furious that we didn't ask him. He made it perfectly clear that friends of the Emir don't buy any damn horses; they get them as a gift from him. Lavish, we though. Send it to us. Said and done, the Emir is a man of his word.

A couple of days later, a guy is standing with a horse outside the compound, trying to get in. We thankfully accept the horse and give him our thanks for his help. I get him to the side discretely and ask him how much money he needs to go home. "I stay here", he said. I stood there like a question mark. After some debate and discussion, we came to the following conclusion:

Mohammed, as his name is, is a slave owned by the Emir.

His family has been slaves for three generations.

He has been with the horse since it was a foal.

He's a stable boy and is part of the Emir's complete package, i.e. if you get a horse you also get a stable boy for free, thus the expression Turnkey Solution.

So, to put it in lesser terms. I own a slave, you own a PlayStation.

GREEK STYLE SOUP

This story is starring Anthony Basil Hadjandonis, also conveniently called ABH in common tongue (no one's able to say his whole name) and his maid Faith, who, well leaves a lot to wish for, or simply makes you have a lot of faith, or lose faith is more accurate, hence the name.

ABH is part of senior management. He's quite an oddball and an eccentric. Of course, he is Greek, with all the things that accompany it, like wearing a golden cross and every time you mention something, you get told that it stems from something from Greece.

Simply put, he's extremely weird. He gets the shivers when he signs cheques or writes on postcards as he experiences it as limiting his personality when he has to write in a "confined space", as he calls it.

He's always at the airport 7 hours before departure. Why? Because he once lived in Lagos where you had to be at the airport early due to the horrible traffic. ABH could have lived in Slough and still be at Heathrow 7 hours before departure. Just in case.

In the canteen, he has a couple of rules of conduct. Since most people eating there are Lebanese, and since he doesn't want to disturb them, he takes a seat at a table where one or two people are sitting, never more.

In principle, he has principles for everything. And that's not all, he's also stubborn as a mule.

ABH always eats his lunch at home - some cheese, a salad or soup. This day, ABH had bought instant soup and asked kindly if Faith could prepare it for lunch, which she of course could. To ensure that she knew what she was doing, ABH asked if she knew how to make instant soup. Of course she knew how to make instant soup.

ABH went about his day, went to the office to put spokes in peoples wheels by being the oddball that he is.

At 12.30, the entire office goes for lunch, apart from ABH that goes at 13.00, because he's done it like that since the 17th century and he will keep doing it like that.

At home, he will enjoy his instant soup and gets it served in a pot. The thing was though, that the hopeless Faith had cooked the instant soup powder with no water, leaving a solidified mess at the bottom of the pan, constructed to survive an earthquake measuring 7,8 on the Richter scale.

You couldn't talk to ABH for the rest of the day. He was furious. I was highly entertained.

I'M ALSO GAY

The legislation that governs homosexuality is just as silly as everything else in Nigeria, which should not surprise you by now. It's characterized by two nice things:

1. Being gay is punished with the death penalty.
2. Thinking a homosexual thought can lead to 5 years in prison.

The first one won't really make you lose your cool right, it's pretty normal in many African countries. The other one on the other hand, takes the cake. If we just ignore the burden of proof, imagine having a nightmare and as part of the nightmare itself, there is a naked man in the background. Do you tell?

With this in mind, fruit cakes seem to make their pilgrimage to Nigeria. I know a few, including a couple who live together where one of them is hired under the pretext that he is a cook. I mean it helps because they have diplomatic immunity, but why not choose another country?

My favorite fudge packer is Mårten. Mårten is a Danish guy who works as GM on Sheraton. The thing is, Mårten isn't our classic "arty gay" but more of a fascist homo. There is something very sadistic over his entire presence – he's acting like a real Nazi. Add to that him trying to mask his gayness with heterosexual attributes that he takes way too far, making his gay attributes shine through. His trick is to surround himself with as many whores as possible in his own hotel. My theory is simple: if you're a John, you don't show it off at your work place. It should be added that me and him dislike each other a lot so I started something I like to call project expulsion. My discontent for him has nothing to do with his sexuality, I just don´t like the man. It´s that simple.

I grabbed Friday, a Ghanaian working at Sheraton as a waiter, and started talking with him with the hope of spreading a fun rumor. I informed Friday that I thought Mårten was gay. Friday rolled over from laughter. The idea of being homosexual was so alien to him that he started walking around, informing each and every one of the guests that he was gay, turned to me and laughed, and the same thing to the staff, and he laughed and laughed.

A week later when I was spending my Saturday by the pool, I asked for Friday. Apparently, he had been deported, for being gay.

Oops, my plan went wrong. To say the least.

ENHANCING LIQUIDITY IN THE TELECOM INDUSTRY

All companies that work in the Telecom industry should have a look at this. In part to learn what doesn't work, but mostly to enhance their liquidity.

Let's start with taking a look at what doesn't work. The whole point of having an address book is that text messages that you send will find the person you want to send it to.

Not in Nigeria though. I many cases, the text messages go to the number you send most of your messages to; in my case the woman I was with at the time.

Luckily, I stayed away from screwing my secretary, so I didn't have the problem of sending the wrong text messages to my woman.

What did happen though was that several text messages consisting of direct orders about how we were to address certain issues, where in God's name people were, how they managed to fuck things up etc., they sure went to her.

It didn't make things better that she eventually gave up on her efforts to inform me that she had received these texts, so thinking that they had received my texts but ignored them, I gave them hell. Of course, they didn't understand anything. Thank you MTN, GLO, Etisalat and all other companies in the telecom industry.

As I've mentioned earlier, you always use two phones in Nigeria. The sole reason is that the coverage is better for some operators in different areas. Or rather, some companies have no coverage at all in some areas.

The second reason is that the companies sometimes, or often, use all kinds of tricks to keep their liquidity in order.

Since invoicing, the mail system, personal identification number and enforcement agencies are completely absent in Nigeria, you can't open an account without depositing money. As soon as this limit is exceeded, the account is shut down until you have deposited more money. The only thing that's cheap in Nigeria is the phone service, so it's physically impossible break the limit - to call for more than 300 pounds per month.

About once a month, when people are getting paid, they shut down the entire telecom network for outgoing messages for one of the companies. Then, you will have to use your other subscription when you need to call someone. You call customer service from your glomobil to mtn (two different service providers). It sounds like this:

   -My phone isn't working.
   -The system is currently offline so I can't see exactly what's wrong,
      but I would guess that you have exceeded your limit. You can

come to the office tomorrow and add 50 000 naira (about £300) and you'll see that it will start working again.
-Thanks, you guys are too cute. (there's no point in arguing anymore)

You do as they say and a couple of days later when the company has been injected with loads of cash, they open the network again and suddenly you can use your account again. Do I even need to add that despite calling, more money gets into the hands of the operator every month, which of course you're never able to access. The song they sing: "due to security reasons, we don't handle cash." On the giving end at least. Accepting cash is never a problem.

I wonder what the CPA would say if BT acted like this?

KEEPING THE REARVIEW MIRROR ATTACHED

Seems obvious to many, and it is. But many existential questions are put to the test in Lagos - the city of cities, or the city of excellence as they call themselves.

Lagos is a nice city for about 3 days, mostly over the weekend. The rest of the time is just pure suffering, and you're spending most of the time in traffic.

Lagos was once the capital of Nigeria, but as it got too crowded, they pulled a classic dictator move and changed the capital to a place that did not exist. At the time at least.

The area of Lagos is pretty much the equivalent of inner city of London, though 18 million people share the space instead of the 3 million that reside in the inner city of London. Some live in luxury, other people live under trucks, but everyone owns a car, no matter how poor or rich you are. All of this is the recipe for disaster.

The traffic in Lagos is one of the most insane things you can experience on earth. You can have two meetings on one day, one at eleven and one at four in the afternoon, with the precondition that you leave your house at seven in the morning. With this in mind, you have to equip your car with some necessities.

1. A mobile internet plan, so you can email from your car.
2. Water, so you can drink.
3. Something to pee in.
4. Chocolate and candy to keep the blood sugar levels high.

The reason for this is that you simply don't leave your car when you're in Lagos, some places are just too dangerous. Due to the extreme poverty levels, you'll get lynched on the spot. Additionally, there's nowhere to go if you leave the car. It's not like there are sidewalks everywhere, so if you leave the car anywhere else than the intended destination, you'll probably be run over before you get lynched. In other words: stay in the car. Pee in a bottle, even though you are ashamed of pulling out your Johnson in front of the driver, who will scornfully ogle you in the rearview mirror.

You might feel safe inside the car, but that doesn't mean that the car is safe. I was honored to experience this first hand when I politely had been in traffic for about an hour, in one and the same spot. A guy on his moped approaches me and starts to loosen my right rearview mirror. I thought it was just too far out, so I felt like I had to be a little bit cool and pulled down the window, just a little bit though, like a coward and said "take the other one too" and thought I was funny. I didn't count on that the guy would take it literally, as he went over to the other side of the car and started loosening the other rearview mirror as well.

FAMILY RELATIONSHIPS

As a newcomer in Nigeria, family relationships can become a bit too much to handle. You quickly realize that the families have a tendency to become quite large and it's not out of the question to come to the conclusion that Nigerian men are stallions. From a reproductive point of view.

Allow me to introduce Lincoln, a driver that grabbed me during my first days in Nigeria. He welcomed me to his country and praised my presence and how much it meant to the country that I was there and how much I would contribute. After the charm offensive, he asked me if I needed to hire some people, his brothers apparently needed work. Sure, I said, just send them over.

For three days I was the cause of mass migration to my office. People sat in the office, in the hallway, sat hidden behind shelves and were in general an inconvenience. I was struck by performance anxiety. I'm 32 years and everything I've managed can be summed up in a couple of abortions. I was ashamed; my manliness disappeared out the window and left standing was a 32 year old man with a boyish look equipped with genitals that apparently was completely useless. I was in chock regarding how many brothers there were. I threw water at myself to wake up from the nightmare, used perfume, smelling salts, but the nightmare wasn't over.

I gathered the courage to ask:

    -Lincoln, are they all really your brothers?
    -Sah, yes Sah! (Sir, yes Sir!)

Damn, I thought, I'm really behind on this, while gasping for air.

I felt really bad and decided to ask around to see if the guys that had been there longer than me could confirm or deny this, and got armed with a question in return. I didn't know if it would work, but my confidence slowly returned to me as my instincts to reproduce grew.

I sat down in my office and called in thirty people at a time with Lincoln there as well. I then pointed at each one of them and asked:

Is this your brother?

    -Yes

Same mother, same father?

> -No, same church, no same town, no same parish, no same tribe, no same mother only, no he is actually my cousin, no, no, no, no, no, no, no and again no.

I had cracked the code. I threw the entire bunch out the door, went to the bathroom, pulled down my pants and had a quick pep-talk with my Johnson. The order was restored.

GETTING RIPPED OFF

I've said it before and I'll say it again: you can never win against a Nigerian, no matter what the issue is. They may be shortsighted, but they always win, no matter how clever you think you are. I'm an intelligent person; there is no doubt about that. I would say so myself, and there is an entire entourage of both friends and enemies that are willing to attest to the same fact. In Nigeria though, I constantly feel stupid and I'm always one step behind.

This is especially true when you catch someone with their fingers in the cookie jar. That's the time you feel at your smartest. But every time, they slide by with some whitewash or a stupid comment that completely disarms you and leaves you standing there, dumbfounded.

Like when stone is disappearing from a quarry. When you load a truck on a quarry, you weigh it before it rolls out. You then message the receiver that Truck X is coming, loaded with 35 tons. "Oh, great" you think. Then Truck X arrives, driven by someone we can call General, that's his name alright? The truck is weighed in, and now it only weighs 28 tons. The guy receiving the truck starts yelling and accuses General for having stolen 8 tons, which he probably did and sold it on the way to make a quick buck. So what's his answer?

> -But Sah, I am a newborn?

I.e. I'm saved (referring to his salvation), so he is Christian.

Suddenly we have a problem. If the guy yelling is a Muslim this is now a religious matter instead of a theft. A lynch mob was created in a flash. So, dumbfounded he quickly leaves the subject and settles for the 28 tons.

Another way of disarming can be to use the classic "right and left". As you might not know, the left side is the side of the devil and thus one of the reasons why you still beat the crap out of your left-handed kids in the Arab world, no matter the religion.

My maid is unable to leave things untouched, so once she stole some money from me. I caught her red-handed and was once again incredibly pleased that this time, there surely can't be an excuse or way to get out of it, I even called the cops.

The police arrived and did the entire interrogation and was really mean to her. After getting yelled at she just said:

-It wasn't me, it was my left hand.
-Oh, why didn't you say so, said the police officer. It was the Devil acting, you shouldn't be punished for that, off you go.

I stood there with my jaw attached to the ground.

It gets even better. A Nigerian CFO managed to do something similar, but in a court case. An American company had made the mistake to let one be the sole signatory for both the company and the cheques. It's called duality in bank lingo when you have to be two to be able to release the mula.

Anyway, this guy was employed for less than a week before he, with no shame in his body, managed to transfer all of the company's funds to his own account.

This was discovered after a few days and the Americans did the only right thing they could do and sued the living hell out of the guy.

In the Supreme Court, he got grilled at the witness stand, but handled himself with flying colours. According to him, he was a good Christian and if God, Jesus or the Holy Ghost (I don't know which one of the trinity that is responsible for money) didn't want him to have the money, he would never had been given the opportunity.

The Nigerian went free, the Americans fainted.

Another guy, called Francis Atuche, or FA as we who now him call him, was alleged of stealing £100 million pounds, from his bank, who later became insolvent, was freed from this ridiculous charges. However this was what he said on the witness stand "I am a catholic, I cannot be a thief. I was baptized in church and before I left primary school I have started to receive Holy Communion, which I do every day. I cannot receive Holy Communion when I am not in a state of grace. I cannot be a thief because God has been gracious to me".

Then of course, there are also attempts that didn't make it to the finish line. Like when the banks hit rock bottom in Nigeria. It turned out that the Chairman for one of the banks had issued a loan to his nanny at £35 million, without collateral. When he got caught, he said that he didn't know how to make a credit check.

Or when our trucks had petrol consumption at more than 100% than normal. We managed to figure out why (by mistake I might add, I just so happened to be passing one of the trucks): a guy was sitting on the tank stealing gas as the truck was in motion, and of course he was in collusion with the driver.

Say what you will about Nigeria, but it's no place for people with pacemakers.

WHY ORDER WILL NEVER BE RESTORED

This story may be true, or it might be made up. Either way, it's highly applicable on Nigeria.

You see, it's an election year. The current president has been in power for 2 terms of office, meaning 8 years, and the people are getting tired of him draining the country of its assets to maintain his apartment in

Paris, screwing blonde models, increasing his collection of Ferraris etc.

Of course, there are a couple of up-and-comers that we usually refer to as the new generation in politics. These are the people who are going to change things, bring new ideas, they are friends with the people, they care about each individual, about everyone's rights, they want to create better welfare, less poverty, greater development, better health care, higher standards of living, education systems that work and that are internationally recognized. These people are the ones that want Nigeria to become a country.

They call these newcomers the ones that care about democracy, and the ones you should vote for in order to get rid of corruption – the things you usually associate with elections in the western world.

The thing is, they have decided that this new candidate, whom we will call "the newcomer", will get a debate USA-style on TV with the current president, the guy that has been in office for two terms, gunning for his third, mano a mano.

D-day comes and the TV debate is under way. Not surprisingly, the entire nation is watching. Not in the American way where everyone is sitting in front of the TV while eating. More like in the developing country way where 50 people are gathered around an oil barrel with a radio sitting on it, alternatively a black and white battery run TV.

The debate begins and the newcomer hits hard with arguments and pretty bold theft allegations. The president is sitting here, not looking very concerned. When the newcomer is finished with his arguments, it's time for the president's rebuttal. Cold as ice, he says:

> -I have indeed stolen money from the country. The first term, I stole for myself, the second term, I stole for my family. This third term, I will steal to give money to you, the people. The newcomer, if he gets elected, will start his first term. What do you think he will do?

Thank you very much, re-elected for a third term in a row.

THE UNION

As in the case of every other country run by gangsters, the union isn't doing the task it's supposed to do, i.e. representing the workers. Instead, their goal is to keep as much capital as possible inside the country, and give the foot soldiers the chance to get their piece of the corruption crumbs. The union also functions like an umbrella organization for harassment and mafia behavior in the style of the American 50's, including illicit distillation, gambling, racketeering etc. Additionally, they are a very strong, popular movement that can be very convincing at negotiations, especially when they don't get what they want. It usually ends with them surrounding offices and other buildings, pouring gasoline everywhere and creating a wall of fire with every employee inside of the ring until they get what they want. Very efficient, but not very TUC-like.

Let's have a look at one of the terms that was negotiated by the union:

11% annual rise in salary, regardless of the results of the company.

After 10 years of service, you get a 14 inch TV.

After 15 years of service, you get a fridge and a freezer.

If you have been forced to move for work, it's the responsibility of the employer to make a contribution to the employee. This contribution is for the entire family, with a maximum of 4 wives and their offspring.

If you're a welder, you get a packet of milk a day, distributed once a month and are meant to help against the fumes. Of course, people sell these to make a buck.

For people who work in dusty areas, you get a monthly "dust allowance" in cash.

Everyone working on the floor gets a two-piece uniform by the employer. We made the mistake of giving our employees one-pieces. We had to stop production for a week – "it says two-piece in the conditions!" Of course, you don't wear these at work but when you go to church.

The chairman of the union gets an official company car by the employer.

Maybe I don't have to say much more?

CHRISTIAN BIGAMY

As long as you're a little bit of a Brainiac, you've probably understood by now that monogamy isn't applicable with a real Nigerian state of mind. It has nothing to do with religion; it's just that Nigerians like to spend time with as many females as possible. Apart from marrying as many as possible, they are having just as many on the side. However, there's a hierarchy to the situation, and it looks something like this:

1. Wife/wives: attend official gatherings where other wives attend as well.
2. Lover/lovers: travel to London and get spoiled with shopping etc.
3. Girlfriend: a combination of the above, but you aren't official.
4. Hookers: for orgies, gangbangs and snake pits.

As a westerner, it becomes a hassle having just one woman. She has to be a different person depending on the social event; you can't present your wife when someone else has brought their girlfriend. That would be rude and is considered bad taste, or a breach of etiquette. You don't bring your wife to a girlfriend event. Additionally, at all times you have to avoid getting invited to number 4 events. It's a chess game that would make the best mathematicians loose track.

From a religious perspective, it's a disaster for Christianity in general, more specifically Catholicism. Christian Nigerians convert to Islam in order to marry more women. To be honest, I don't really get it. Islam cap it at 4 women but that won't stop them from marrying 10, 20 or 30. Maybe they just need Islam to get the ball rolling, I don't know.

As the pope realized that he was losing ground, he realized that they had to do something drastic. He has allowed Nigerian Catholics to marry 4 women, by allowing one church wedding while the rest are civil. It might just be the most revolutionary thing that has happened in Catholicism in 400 years.

The thing is though; Nigerians are smarter than the Pope. The Muslims that are married with 4 women are converting to Christianity to marry four more, and claim that the first 4 was from when they were Muslims, while the others are Christians and Christians that are married with one woman hastily marry three more, then convert to Islam to marry an additional four with the same argument.

Let's create a simple mathematical formula to make this clearer:

Muslim + 4 women = Convert to Christianity (marry 4 more women) = 1 man married to 8 women.

Christian married to one woman + 3 more women = 4 women = convert to Islam (marry 4 more women) = 1 man married to 8 women.

It's just wonderful.

WHO WEARS THE PANTS AT HOME?

With all of this talk about Johns, prostitution, men getting married with an obscene amount of women, you might have gotten the impression that Nigeria is a country where men are in charge and where women are walking around having to tag along according to the whims of the men. Once again, this would be a mistake. Nigerian men are more pussy whipped than the average man. Additionally, the women are very scary if they decide to get angry. I like to go out and scream a little at any Nigerian man, for example in traffic, but if I get crossed with a Nigerian woman, I will stay put in the car, paralyzed from fear.

One example from real life:

A diesel provider that we work with is unexpectedly run by a woman.

Women are in general more diligent than men I would say, they are the ones that bring home the bacon, while men are sitting around, acting like windbags and trying to figure out the next scam that will make them multimillionaires, while getting drunk. Do you know that saying "If wealth was the inevitable result of hard work and enterprise, every woman in Africa would be a millionaire"? Well, it´s true.

The line of business might feel a little bit surprising; what's even more surprising is that she actually has a pretty large business compared to other businesses in Nigeria. She would place well on the stock exchange in a European country. She is illiterate by the way.

Additionally, she's everywhere in the company, and will help out a bit here and there as she pleases. This day she drove the truck to the site to deliver Diesel to our construction site. Apparently, superwoman has a truck license as well. Maybe she doesn't but at least she can drive it.

When we were getting ready to receive the delivery, it dawned on us that she had cheated with the quality. She wants to get paid for premium when it obviously isn't, and to top it off the volume is 20% less than agreed but she still wants to get paid in full. (You mix diesel with water to increase your profit).

Of course, our guys don't want to receive the delivery, and a riot breaks out where people are yelling, screaming, taunting each other etc.

In the middle of the commotion the guy responsible at the construction site arrives to "handle" the problem. He's a tough Lebanese guy that won't get scared by either a woman or a Nigerian, or the combination of the two.

He explained to her in a male chauvinist pig manner that only Lebanese men can muster that she should get her stuff and get the hell out of there.

Just as he finishes his sentence, proud of having handled the situation, this old lady leans back and then launches her skull right at his nose, breaking it and choking him with his own blood.

We received her delivery on her terms and conditions.

The humiliation was complete, and we still don't dare to order diesel from anyone else, despite us getting cheated every time.

Terror and fear is very effective.

MY WONDERFUL ASSISTANT BECKY

Her main task is to keep my blood pressure high and to make sure that my heart is beating unevenly.

I have failed in a spectacular way to educate her into doing anything sensible, and even less in having any kind of control over her.

The point in having Becky is to make my work easier. Unfortunately, I have to look at every little thing she's doing, and instead of making my work easier, she's consistently adding 4 extra hours to my days, where I meticulously have to check up on her work. When you're looking for errors, it's easy to become blind after a while and every time you control her work, you miss more stuff. One time I asked her to issue a cheque for 10,000 pounds to some company. I got the cheque back and thought that everything seemed to be in order, signed it and sent it to the bank. 3 hours later, the bank lets me know that they are missing both the currency we are asking for and that we have insufficient funds to cover the payment. Of course, I gave the bank manager a scolding. He hands over the cheque without saying a word. I glance at it quickly and soon realize that Becky is a rising star like no other. It says:

10,000,000.00 Ponds.

Ten million ponds, instead of ten thousand pounds.

He looks at me and says: "Sir, I have never dealt with ponds in my entire life"

I've also caught Becky sleeping at work on two different occasions. She's managed to escape unscaved both times. One time I was yelling at her, full force "Are you sleeping at work!?"

No no, she answers, I'm looking at the floor.

So if I say that she can't look at the floor, she will walk around starring at the ceiling all day and claim that she can't work because if she does, there's a chance that she will look at the floor by mistake, failing to work according to my directives.

The other time I caught her, I said the same thing. This time, I got this as the reply:

"I'm praying".

Once again, completely outmaneuvered. If I would say that she can't pray, it would suddenly be about religion and not her shortcomings in the workplace.

You can never win against a Nigerian.

KILICHI

My first encounter with Nigerian snacks is, to say the least, bitter sweet. To this day, I still don't know if I like kilichi, or if it was something else.

Kilichi is a meat snack made from dried beef drenched in Nigerian pepper. I tagged along with my cousin, to a prominent Nigerian to welcome me to Nigeria.

I had just had a little taste of kilichi and was craving more; I thought it was really damn good and wanted to try it again. The jungle telegraph had reached our beloved prominent Nigerian, and in the name of hospitality he had prepared some homemade kilichi for me.

We sat down, and since this was my first meeting with a Nigerian family in their home environment, I was probably a little bit cautious as I wasn't completely confident in their customs. To be honest, I had no idea about their customs.

We sat down and started chit-chatting, you know, like you do with strangers about this and that and everything and nothing. At this time, I didn't know that it was appropriate for the guest to reach for snacks or if the guest should wait to get served. I would soon find out.

The phone of the prominent Nigerian started ringing, and apparently it's totally fine to answer the phone without considering your guests. Apparently it's also fine to speak so loud that every little detail of the conversation is shared with your guests. During the call, I'm starring at the kilichi, sitting there at the table, feeling like it's almost talking to me. It wants me to eat it…

During the call the Nigerian is struck by a scratch attack and decides to act in full force by running down his entire hand into the back of his pants, probably under his underwear, and starts scratching so loudly that you can hear the sound of nails against skin, while he at the same time is yelling at the phone.

Suddenly, he takes his hand out of his pants, breaks a piece of Kilichi with the same hands that said hello to his buttocks, and gives it to me. I froze, but thawed back to life again as a family member kicks me under the table, saying "Eat. Now."

Reluctantly, I grab this piece of kilichi, spiced up with the taste of his buttocks and starts going to town on it.

The issue is that I like it. Do I like the taste of kilichi or do I like the taste of male buttocks?

Another existential question for me to ponder.

MANANA

The Nigerians have their own way of procrastinating things. Everyone is familiar with the Spaniard's manâna as a way of postponing the stuff you can do today and do them tomorrow in order to have a siesta or drink sangria.

The Spaniard's way of manâna isn't that great though, as the problem never goes away. You say that you will do it, just not today, and you keep putting it off as long as you can, but you never get rid of the problem if you don't start working on it, or until the client gets tired of you.

Since Nigeria is built on delayed deliveries, broken promises and half-measures, it's very important to disclaim yourself from all responsibility. You know, like the clause you see in some contracts, that you can't be held responsible in the case of terrorist attacks, earthquakes and other extreme situations, the thing that's called force majeure.

No one wants expose themselves to the guillotine.

They have solved this with one simple sentence that they use to answer all questions and that fulfills all of the criteria above:

-When will the crane arrive?
-Any moment from now.

-Did you call the supplier and ask for the delivery?
-I am on top of the matter.

> The following exchange took place between me and my driver. He was out on an errand on my behalf, and I needed to know when he was back, so I could start going home.
>
> Me: Igwe, we u dey? (Igwe, where are you?)
> Igwe: Oga, a de come. (I am on my way).
> Me: Igwe, we u dey? (Igwe, where are you?)
> Igwe: A de around. (I am close by).
> Me: Igwe, we u dey? (Igwe, where are you?)

Igwe: On my way coming.
Me: Igwe, wen u go reach office? (Igwe, when will arrive?)
Igwe: Oga, any moment from now.

At this stage, I understood that he was not going to reply to my question, so I opted for a new strategy and tried to get some sense of where he was by trying to get a landmark of sort.

Me: Igwe, wettin u de see? (What do you see?).

He paused for half a minute and then replied:

Oga, a see sky. (I see the sky).

AKIN IS IN NEED OF MONEY

Since Akin is my driver, I'm what people call his Master, i.e. the one that has to take care of him whether I like it or not. As a Master, my commitments can be summarized into one: acting like a bank when his pockets are empty. I might need to add that this happens quite often. With a salary of a couple of hundred pounds per month, I have to add a bit of extra money quite often, pay for school for four kids, the rent for the house, some medicine etc.

You might be thinking that they should have higher wages instead, but that won't stop these guys from asking for money, and also, it's a good way of creating a loyal relationship with the drivers which will make it less likely for me to get kidnapped.

You can split my commitments into two parts; when he really needs my help and when he just wants some extra money in his pockets. Let's not kid ourselves; he's probably exaggerating when he really needs help as well, but still.

Really though, it's part two that's the most interesting, because it's here that he will add a sneering, almost mocking smile, which means something like: "Both you and me know that I'm lying, but you're going to give me the dough anyway so why are we doing this dance?". To add to that, he's not even very good in making an effort.

One day, he enters my office with puppy eyes in combination with that sneering smile. I knew what would come, but I didn't know how unprepared he was.

>   -Akin, what do you want?
>   -Masta
>   -Mmmm
>   -I need help, the children burned down and the house have to go to school.

Without even looking at him, I keep on working and simultaneously inform him that his lie was horrible. It should be something along the lines of that the house is on fire and that the children need to go to school.

I gave him a paper and a pen, asked him to go away for half an hour, hone his lying craft and then return to show me what he could do.

Do you think he came up with something good? No. Do you think he got money from me? Yes.

HOW MUCH IS HUMAN LIFE WORTH?

A very interesting question, but first, we'll have to have look at what we're dealing with. 150 million people. Every sixth African is a Nigerian. Family constellations that look like Ponzi schemes. 70% poverty despite a good GDP.

Anyway, I'm relatively new to Abuja and have just started to drive the car myself every now and then, primarily on nights and Sundays when the drivers don't work.

I'm putting the pedal to the metal accompanied to some sweet tunes as I roam the Abuja freeways, singing along and picking my nose - the things you do when you're driving by yourself. A bit further ahead, I see two people on the side of the road where one of them seems to be holding on to the other as he can't stand by his own accord.

I quickly make the assessment that they won't try to run across the road, and I'm right. What I didn't account for was that the person who was holding on to the other would throw the other guy in front of my car, mashing him to pieces, killing him on the spot.

I jump out of the car, and he approaches me saying I killed his father, that I should watch myself, that I'm a guest in his country etc. A gang joins in and suddenly, I'm surrounded by a group of 50 or so Nigerians screaming at me, wanting to kill me.

I manage to squeeze out that I'm certainly willing to compensate the family for the assassination and do right by me.

The lynch mob calms down instantly, as if I said the magical words and I immediately start negotiating with the son. After some wealing and dealing like on the Manchester flea-market, we came to the understanding that his father's life was worth at most 100 pounds. We shook hands and he got paid.

The lynch mob scattered and I composed myself to ask the question I wanted to ask to begin with. I asked him: "why did you throw your father in front of my car?"

> -Well, he said, he's 83 years old and very sick. This way, he died an honorable death, supporting his family instead of costing them a fortune. That's good right?

LAGOS DOMESTIC AIRPORT

The Lagos Domestic Airport is definitely in a league of its own. The entire building is like 100 square meters and to maximize the area, they have demolished a whole lot of doors on the side so you are being lead outside and in, and the out on the other end, standing there waiting, and then in, then out etc.

It begins at the check in. Here it's all about trying to stand on top of people in order to get into the line, even though you have a ticket. If you've got some luggage, you're screwed if you haven't checked in on time.

If you're lucky you receive your boarding card, hand written of course, and if you're me you've also received a name change to something more African:

Hatem Sababaga.

The fact that it didn't match my Nigerian driver's license was not an issue to anyone.

When you've fought your way through security, you are standing in front of all the gates and this is where the exciting part begins. There's no board with arrivals and departures. Instead they use a big speaker where they call out the flights. Unfortunately, they blew out the treble 20 years ago and maxed the bass. Additionally, the call outs are made in Pidgin, so of course you don't understand anything. And that goes for the Nigerians as well.

The only way of guaranteeing that you make your flight is to run out on the runway every time a plane is landing and ask where it's coming from and where it's going. To Benin you say? Do you know when the Abuja flight is landing? I think it's on runway 4.

So you run with all you've got to runway 4, only to find out that your flight isn't there. You keep doing this until you're on the right airplane.

DRINKING AS A MUSLIM ALTERNATIVELY NOT DRINKING AS CHRISTIAN

The above should not compute, of course, but in a strange way, it does. The following text should put theology to the test. We're at a dinner party where I'm one of the guests. The other guests aren't very important, but one of them sticks out: Chief Abu, our new chairman that took over after the death of his father. Chief Abu is a Muslim. His wife, whose name I can't recall, is a Christian and his brother in law is a Christian as well.

Before we sit down at the table we decide to grab a drink before the meal, so we pour a big glass of wine each. Chief Abu drinks like a cesspool despite his religion, so he gets a really big one, as does his wife.

Of course, I think that the brother in law is a drunk as well so I pour him a big one too and hand him the glass. Chief Abu's wife dives across the room and grabs the glass in the middle of the air, looks angrily at me and says: "he can't drink, he's a Christian!"

She says that while wielding a glass of red wine in her hand, and at the same time Chief Abu is standing next to her pounding down the entire glass of wine.

Could someone please explain to me how this works from a religious point of view?

LOVE ME LOVE YOU/MONEY WOMAN

In England you can choose to get married in church or do a civil marriage, or both. In Nigeria, more specifically in Obudu, close to the Cameroonian border, you have two completely different alternatives.

Let's start with the first one: "Love me, love you". Just like it sounds, it's based on love. Since this kind of marriage is based on feelings, you're allowed to divorce if the feelings go away. You might think that it's only possible for the man to break things off, but that's not the case, it's primarily for the women.

In the "concept" of "Love me, love you" a small dowry is required to give to the father, as the risk of the girl leaving is looked upon as relatively low. Despite this, "Love me, love you" marriages are great from an economical point of view as you get some money when you get married, keep it when you get divorced and you're free to remarry when you need to make bank again.

"Money woman" is more hardcore. The dowry is a lot more significant, reaching 2 annual salaries. But it also means that the ownership has changed from the father to you and that the woman now is your property. If she would decide to pack her stuff and leave, the father will not only have a hard time marrying off his other daughters, it also means that he will have to give back the dowry and an additional fine.

If she misbehaves, or acts in a way you don't deem appropriate, you can execute her and bury her. Since she's a "money woman", she belongs to you and what you do with her is not controlled by law. It's a bit like scrapping your car, according to this guy.

Who's up for lobbying for some new laws in England?

FAITH TABERNACLE

Is the biggest church (documented by the Guinness book of world records) in the world. It can fit 50,000 people on the inside, and an additional 300,000 people outside. It's filled to the brim on Sundays. The Obasanjo (ex-president/military ruler) chicken farm is right next to the church.

The church is a part of the umbrella organization called Winners Chapel. Apart from Faith Tabernacle, they have 300 churches all over Nigeria, and subsidiaries in 32 African countries, Dubai, England and USA.

Faith Tabernacle is also broadcasting their Sunday services worldwide in channels such as the God Channel.

Other operations within the organization include 4 banks, completely owned by Winners Chapel.

All of this is owned and run by Pastor Oyedepo.

Let's have a look at his financial statements, but to keep it simple we'll only be looking at Faith Tabernacle. After having looked at our locals books, I noticed that every Nigerian donate about 25% of what the make to the church. So let's count on the downside and say that the average salary is £100, i.e., you donate £25 to the church, every month. That means that the pastor will get £8,750,000 per month only counting one of the churches – one of the "factories".

The pastor is living it up in Italian tailor made suits, bespoke shoes, Italian sports cars and last but not least, as a man of god and of the people, two private jets (he had to sell one of them though a couple of years ago). No one looks twice at this, of course. As the man of God man of the people he is supposed to fly private. His net worth was estimated by Forbes to 150 Million USD in 2011.

I should've become a pastor.

TELEPHONY FOR A BARGAIN

Apparently, we have an analogue line somewhere collecting dust that no one seems to care about as it's not working.

One day, out of the blue, we received a phone bill demanding £40,000.

No one had a clue that we could even receive an analogue bill, even less that we had a working line, or that the analogue network was working in the first place.

It was our first thought that the phone company was trying to screw us, but they even showed us a specification of the calls that were made, so we had to realize that the error somehow was on our part.

We brought out old maps and blueprints and realized that there was an old line going through the basement, but we didn't quite understand what was going on.

When night came, we put up cameras and microphones in the basement so we could monitor the situation.

The day after, we found out that one of our locals is connecting to the phone line and is selling international calls to bargain prices. The fun thing is how he set the prices. The telephony in Nigeria is being controlled by supply and demand, i.e. it's cheap to call to USA since many people call there, but it costs a fortune to call to Ghana as no one want to call the people living there. This guy set prices based on distance. Oh, you're calling the states? That's far away so you'll have to pay this and that, and you're calling the Ivory Coast? Well, this time it's on me as you've called there so many times and as it's so close to Nigeria it won't cost that much.

We enjoyed the spectacle for a bit, and then we made sure he got a punch up the bracket.

SHOPLIFTING A QUARRY

Even if you're not in the construction business it's pretty easy to imagine what a quarry looks like. You've got a giant machine crushing granite. Additionally, it's sitting in one and the same spot the entire time, with loads of conveyor belts that are supposed to transport rocks basically everywhere.

Setting up a quarry takes about 3-4 weeks with a man power of about 120 people. At least in Nigeria – in England you can get 12 people to the same job in the same time frame with a working week of 6 days.

One day, one of our employees came to work only to see that their work place was gone.

In less than 12 hours, from dusk to dawn, they had managed to disassemble the whole site.

This is not a game my dear friends. We're talking about thousands of tons of bulky steel and bulky parts.

We'll have to assume that the people who did this were extremely motivated, and that the guards that were supposed to make sure something like this couldn't happen were in on it.

I sat down and tried to calculate the manpower needed for a project like this. I reached the conclusion that it took 1,300 people and 50 trucks to finish the job in 12 hours.

That's impressive, even though the wallet took a beating.

RADIO PERMIT IN THE CAR

I just got a fine for not having a radio permit in the car. You might ask yourself, is this really a thing or is it a blatant scam? After some careful research, it appears that this is actually a real thing. You can have a stereo in the car, but you're not allowed to listen to it if you don't have a radio permit.

What's astonishing is that I got stopped by the police. Police might be a strong word; it's actually the youth squad from the union acting like police, i.e. local gangsters. Area boys plain and simple.

They just launched a spike strip in front of the car, forcing me to brake in panic. In the middle of the commotion that broke out, people start to surround the car, making it impossible to move in either direction.

As the chaos settles and you start to get an idea how to maneuver away from the situation, a guy comes towards you, smirking, with your registration plates in his hands.

Of course, I made a scene, hurling all kinds of threats in their direction. To no avail. Two hours later, I had to pay the fine, but also buy back my plates. Three or four of the dummies asked me to come over and started to talk to me until I gave them a price that they were happy with. I was ready to cry when I had got my plates back, and my freedom. My dignity on the other hand, was left where I got stopped.

NIGERIAN CATERING SERVICES

More particularly, we're talking about a business run by four females. Not a great idea, it would show and Abuja Hashers got to experience this first hand. I joined this group of people who had taken upon themselves to organize walks in nature every other Saturday. I must admit that my only reason to join was to flirt with the ladies. The flirting was a disaster, so was the walk and all the other participants too. There was no one there I wanted to spend time with.

A cool thing happened afterwards though. After the walk, everyone gathered for something to eat and drink. I saw a light at the end of the tunnel, the opportunity to get drunk in order to get something out of these social freaks.

To celebrate this special day, they had organized a catering business consisting of four Nigerian women cooking Nigerian food.

Just as people were getting chatty with each other, the women suddenly started flipping out on each other. To this day, no one still knows why. They went bananas/ape-shit, Ricky Lake/Jerry Springer style. One of the girls grabs the table and flips it, making food rain down on my colleague only to be followed by a second girl grabbing 20 dinner plates smashing them on the other girl's skull making her fall like a leaf to the ground.

In comes the last girl, slashes off the neck of the bottle and cuts herself in the arm to show that she's not scared. Then, she marshes against the woman that used the plates as a weapon.

The host tried to break them apart, and got smashed by a bottle to the face. The guards finally took action and starting waving with their batons until the girls were on the ground, and everyone tried to join in to end the chaos.

Everyone, except me. I had decided to enjoy the highlight of the day, without risking my life. After all, it's worth a whole lot more than most.

WETTIN U BRING FOR ME?

That's a phrase you hear every time you reach the airport. You get a bit stunned the first time and try to squeeze on by with some witty comment. I decided to try one that I really believed in. Most people who approach you happen to be standing under the EFCC sign. EFCC is the anti-corruption authority. They have a slogan that says something like "watch out for corruption, don't nurture it". It was an appropriate place for my move.

I thought I was being really clever that used it as cover. Surely, you're not standing here, under the EFCC sign and demand a bribe, I barked with as much authority as I could muster. He screamed back that it's not a bribe, it's a present.

Put in my place, again. It took a couple of trips before I could fine tune my one-liner, and at last, I actually hit home. I didn't just slip by; I also managed to blame it all on the British. Win-win for me.

After landing, I get the default question once again: "Sah, wetting you bring for me?"

"Oh man, I bought some tax free stuff for you at Heathrow, but the Brits told me I couldn't bring it on the plane!"

His answer: "Colonial bastards."

Goootchaa!

AIRPORT SECURITY

How to stay above the law is a common topic of conversation in Nigeria. And a highly important one. We have an employee called Harry whose job is to check in people who are traveling abroad and then bring them home when they get back.

The procedure works like this: Harry takes your passport, luggage and the ticket the day prior to the flight and then goes to the airport by himself. He will check you in, tag your luggage, put a stamp in your passport and gets your boarding card.

The day after, you go about an hour before departure and meet up with Harry, or rather Harry meets you at the flight about 20 minutes before departure. You go straight through security where Harry says hi to a group of people and exchange a couple of pleasantries and cash. You swoosh past customs, up the stairs, walk past everyone scanning their boarding cards and get escorted to the airplane doors where you are first on the plane, no matter how many are standing in line.

The way back is even smoother. You step out of the plane where Harry is standing, you give him your passport and you luggage tags and then go straight out of the airport with Harry one step behind you, yelling at a couple of officials that everything's in order. Then you get into the car and fall asleep.

20 minutes later Harry arrives with a stamped passport and your luggage. All well and done. Something to have in mind the next time you think they have meticulous security checks in the west. There's a reason for it.

QUOTE FROM THE DAILY SUN

"Man Caught having sex with donkey

A middle-aged man identified simply as Anayochukwu was stripped by villagers for allegedly having sex with a donkey.

Anayochukwu who hails from Umujovu, Eha-Amufu was handed over to the police after he was paraded naked around the town of Eha-Amufu following a report made by owner of the donkey, Mrs. Nnedi Moses(...)when she caught the suspect forcing his manhood into the donkey. She expressed suspicion that he might have contracted HIV and was looking for a way to spread the scourge. The PPRO said the suspect had confessed to the crime but had asked for pardon as he did not commit it out of his own volition but was influenced by demonic forces."

Daily Sun, Tuesday, October 2, 2012

FACEBOOK

I found this post on Facebook, it speaks for itself.

Elisabeth's status: As some of you have noticed, I recently "liked" several churches and religious pages and Jesus himself. This was Rasim being super hilarious. Well thank you Rasim, because one of those churches was a Nigerian Evangelical Church, and from them alone I have had NINETY SEVEN friend requests and FIFTY messages all saying the same thing (I was aware I was blond and Scottish but now I know God loves me! They love me! I love Jesus! We are blessed) and since I was clever enough to put my number on Facebook I've also had a grand total of 145 phone calls and 40 texts, but most of them where from the same guy. All in all there was 12 marriage proposals dispersed, but again 6 of them was from the same guy. And the lesson is? I know I'll be a popular girl in Nigeria, and I need tighter privacy settings.

Adam comment: How I wish I could like this twice.

Elisabeth's reply: it's so painfully annoying, in the middle of the night my phone starts buzzing with notifications and I wake up panicked like "what's the emergency", and there is none, just some guy called Olumide thinks I'll be a perfect wife. Thanks Ollie, but GO AWAY.

REVITALISED BLOG

Somewhere around this time, I decided to start blogging again. Well I did not decide by myself really, but you will understand upon reading the next post. Why this has any significance will become clearer with time.

FIRST NEW/OLD POST

Since my book have become immensely popular, the only correct decision is to resume my blogging, in order to increase sales, and await the Hollywood film contract. A business decision that is based on facts, and facts only.

That´s what you think. Emilia said "Hatem start blogging again". Now, Emilia is a piece of Polish skirt, aged 19, and makes Izabella Scorupco look like Pomperipossa. I am a 33-year old man, with a dirty mind, so my only rational response was "I am on it". I mean, who am I really kidding? I have never based any of my decisions on rationality or facts. I prefer emotional decisions, what I refer to as my "gut feeling". That is another way of saying that I think with my genitalia. Which have always backfired. But sooner or later, it will work for me instead of against me. Either way, that's is not the point of this post, it´s merely an introduction to the same.

Let´s start with introducing our stars of this specific post. The first star is a random Nigerian man in his early forties. The second star, is a Swedish friend of mine, that we can call Eric.

Eric is a very good friend of mine. He is also a hypocrite of enormous proportions. He is born in Africa, and has spent most of his life outside Sweden. His ties to Sweden are therefore minimal. Which means that he does not pay taxes in Sweden, and has no part of the benefits that the system provides. His salary is in line with Botswana's GDP, and is mostly paid to him, through various off-shore companies, to tax havens. In spite of all that, he is a left wing, and throws around Marxist punch lines as if they were candy like "solidarity to help the weak is important for any society". Now the fact that his funds are never close to being part of the welfare system in any country does not seem to bother him at all. And just after a Marxist nugget like that he often follows it up with remarks about fulfilling his need to buy a Malibu beach house. He is full of it basically.

Now Eric works as CFO for a Nigerian company that is listed on the stock market. The company is founded by Lebanese, and with many power Nigerians involved one way or the other. Now his job is to make life miserable for his co-workers, by demanding honesty, transparency, ethics and moral. He is at the wrong place, at the wrong time. And he is a pain in the arse for the cocossion of Nigerians and Lebanese.

The company had its annual general meeting, with its board, and shareholders present. Since these ordeals are quite long, you usually serve food of some sort to keep peoples blood sugar levels up. They also gave away goodie bags with calendars, calculators, and all sorts of garbage with the company logo. At this stage, nothing is out of the ordinary. The circus starts the day after.

Eric, comes to work the day after, and notices that his office is barricaded by a Power Nigerian, who is voicing his discontent for missing yesterday's AGM. Loudly. He refuses to leave Eric's office without receiving his goodie bag. Upon receiving his goodie bag, he also complains that there was food yesterday, and that he has the right to his share. After all, he is a massive shareholder. So Eric arranged for a 7£ food allowance. Then he left.

And Eric decided to check how big of a shareholder he really was. He owned shares for 42 pence. And received a food allowance around 30 times that. Amazing.

GIVING POWER INSTRUCTIONS TO THE MAID

Me: Lilian, boil some pasta for me (with a stern voice).

Lilian: Yes Master.

Result: 1 kg boiled spaghetti for 1 person.

Once again, I fail miserably in giving clear instructions.

BUYING FISH AT THE LOCAL MARKET

At this stage, you must have come to the same conclusion that I have, even if you disagree with it, that I am my own biggest fan. And of the opinion that whatever I touch, turns into gold.

Since I am such a prodigy going to market is something I master. It gives me a sense of being in tune with the people. Another one of my fantastic abilities is to negotiate, which I like to do (I am actually useless at that as well).

Anyway, I find the jumbo prawns that I want, and start negotiating. The lady wants approximately ten pounds per kilo. My counter offer is two pounds. She looks at me with disdain, and in quite a threatening manner. I back off, and give her a new counter. And we go of, and on until we settle for five pounds per kilo. So I buy my two kilos and proudly head home.

Upon reaching my house, I make sure to weigh my goods again to ensure their weight. The scale shows two kilos. Amazing. I open up the bag, and find one kilo of prawns, and a kilo of ice.

Job well done Hatem. Very well done.

FEMI OTEDOLA

Femi is a former rascal, who used to run an old printing press from a shack in Lagos, and used to get most of his jobs by begging and pleading. Femi's father used to be a governor in Lagos, and managed to get him into one of the oil company's as an executive of some sorts about thirteen years ago.

Femi quickly arranged for a coup and took control over the company. He then set up a new company and basically emptied the old one from all its assets. Embezzlement and fraud as it's best.

He is mostly seen on his 50 £ million yacht, dressed in his white outfit, that looks like a pair of pajamas.

Not everybody is happy though. Especially not the embezzled parties. I found this in a Nigerian newspaper, in 2011.

"That's when the problems began: Femi ruined the company. He embezzled the company's funds to the tune of hundreds of millions dollars, and made the company operate at a loss. The company's stock is now trading at an all-time low, and the shareholders have not been paid dividends for two years now. **Shareholders hates his guts for this. Some wish his penis will grow shorter**".

There you have it folks. The hardest most severe punishment, for any African male. A shorter penis.

Although his penis is or at least might be, shorter nowadays, Forbes ranks his net worth to 1.9 Billion USD. So he can probably afford an enlargement.

SLIPPERY SLOPE

A friend of mine went to a local hospital to treat her malaria. She slipped in the middle of the hallway, on her way to the Doctors office.

I know what you are thinking. "What is a banana peel doing in the floor, in a hospital?"

Well, you are wrong. It was no banana peel, but a placenta.

THE NIGERIAN STOCK EXCHANGE

The NSE is as mesmerizing as everything else. Depending on how you count, or who is counting, it is the biggest in Africa. Let's just say that it is one of the top three, which are the Egyptian and the South African stock market.

In total we are talking of about 180 companies. Most of the stocks are not floated at all. No buying and selling if you are not into financial lingo. The Dangote group with its various companies are listed, and they are quite a big chunk of the stock exchange. The Majority owner of the conglomerate is Aliko Dangote, whose net worth is estimated to 18$ Billion by Forbes.

Guess who is the chairman of the Nigerian Stock Exchange? Yes, Mr. Aliko Dangote.

Conflict of interest? There is no such thing in Nigeria.

LAGOS INTERNATIONAL AIRPORT IS CLOSED

Why do you think that is? Snow storm? Terrorist threat?

Once again, you are horribly wrong. The airport was closed because of a case of suspected black magic.

THE TOMATE PASTE FACTORY IN GOMBE

Nigeria has the world's highest defabrication paste. That is not really a word, I think I just invented it. But basically it means that the few factories that exists are shutting down and production is moved elsewhere. Mainly because of 2 things. Nigerians are meatheads. And we do not have sufficient and reliable power sources. To put in terms you understand. We run on diesel generators 24/7. We have no electricity. It's that simple.

In the midst of a factory exodus, Gombe's governor decided to do the exact opposite. He set up a tomato paste factory, that have been operating for five years. He is now looking for an investment of 10$ Million to bump up production.

He hears about my friend Eric, and lures him over with the prospect of Billions to be made ahead.

Eric visits the factory and takes notice of terrifying fact. The place is brand new, everything is shining. There is, nor have there ever been any production what so ever. So he asked for the production figures. And received replies that dealt with maximum capacity, not actual. After pushing for a couple of hours, he got the answer that he wanted or suspected. The factory has produced zero units of tomato paste. The reason for that is that the factory had no electrical supply. It is supposed to run on water turbines, and the closest water source is 80 kilometers away.

My meathead argument still stands.

BLOG SHUT DOWN

After a couple of weeks of blogging, my book and blog caught the eye of the SSS, which is the Nigerian State Security Service-the equivalent of the MI5 or the FBI. A not so good move from a survival perspective, especially if you reside in Nigeria, as I did at the time.

The presiding agency to the SSS was the NSO-National Security Organization. The Director General of the NSO during the eighties was General Gusau, who in the early nineties became the Chief of Army Staff. After his short tenure as Chief of Army Staff he became the National Security Advisor for a total of 7 consecutive years. And an additional year after that. The SSS is the National Security Advisors responsibility.

By 2014 General Gusau was the Minister of Defense. This is by no means bragging on my part. This is to make it clear that the General is an intelligence heavy weight, with very little regards for my human rights, or my life and wellbeing either for that matter.

I got summoned to his office, and picked up by a military convoy. I had no clue if I would come back alive. I have met the General many times before, even at his best, he is intimidating.

He sat me down, and gave me a proper display of his power. He said, without losing his cool, or his smile, and while being extremely polite, that he appreciated my God-given skills as an amazing writer, and complemented me for my detailed descriptions of Nigeria and its people. He also told me that he have had parts of the book and the blog translated and he enjoyed it a lot. However, my sarcasm was not shared by everybody.

In power language this translates to "Stop blogging or I will have you executed".

So, I stopped.

THE ART OF CORPORATE WITCHCRAFT

I have found, that the best way to settle disputes is by staying as far away from the heat as possible. This requires of course someone else to do my dirty work. For optimum results, and swift execution, I have found that my Jojjo is the absolute best remedy. A Jojjo is a medicine man to use western terms, who does black magic, curses people, and finds out the "truth". Highly effective. It´s a bunch of humbug, but they believe in witch craft so it works (for me or to my advantage, and that it was counts). I have had chickens slaughtered in my office, as the blood, when it splashes will point towards the direction of the liar. Things like that. My corporate Jojjo is on a monthly retainer, very much like a barrister. And gets additional payment for each specific task. This is to say that I am quite familiar and comfortable with the art of Black Magic.

Emilia on the other hand is not. Emilia is the kind of person who never feels harassed if you call multiple times, send emails, and multiple texts. Or marriage proposals for that matter. She would have never reacted like Elisabeth. If she´s not up for it, at that specific moment, you might as well stop. Now like everybody else, she thinks that she can combat the Nigerian spirit with her stubbornness. So, on her way home one day while studying in Aberdeen, a Nigerian, named Akim, tried to hit on her, without really giving up. In the end she gave up, and gave him her phone number, with the intention of just ignoring him. Huge mistake. He kept calling, on a daily basis. When she was asleep, he sent so many texts, that she had to start everyday by deleting messages to make room for friends and family to contact her. As there was not just enough memory. She came to me in despair. And I told her what to do. She scorned at me, even flat out laughed in my face. And thought I was mad. After a couple of weeks, she was desperate, and opted for my strategy. Not because she thought it would work, but because she was on the brink of suicide. She sent him the following text:

"Akim, if you won´t leave me alone, Hatem will speak to his Jojjo, and he will cast a spell on you".

Akim replies in an instant. "I am sorry". She never heard of him again.

Oh ye, of little faith.

A DON CHOP DAT BLACK TIN

A good friend of mine, decided to spend Christmas in Verbier. To enhance the pleasure of his stay, he brought his nanny a long so she could keep an eye out on his and his wife's newborn son.

Upon checking in, and getting settled in the room, he noticed that the hotel offered complimentary beluga. Which is a nice touch.

After two days he decided to check up on the nanny, as she had her own room, together with the child. Just to make sure she was alright, it was her first time outside Nigeria after all. So he asked her if she was alright, and if she enjoyed the food that room service provided. She said:

"Oga, dat tin dey sweet me o, no bi lie, a don chopam". She had been eating beluga for 2 days, for breakfast, lunch and dinner. In extreme quantities.

Her bill was over 10 000 dollars.

WELCOME TO PORT HARCOURT

Some of the Arik flights from Port Harcourt to Abuja, just touch down in the capital, before taking off again, and flying to London. A friend was traveling in the height of dry season (so mid-December), wearing shorts, beach foot wear, with local currency and a Nigerian driver's license in his pocket, from Port Harcourt to Abuja. He fell asleep on the plane, and woke up in Heathrow airport. Dressed for a holiday in the Caribbean. With no means to identify himself, or money that he can actually exchange (the naira is a closed currency).

He approached immigration, and tried to stutter out a few words, but had no clue how to frame the issue. Immigration just looked at him wearing shorts, and sighed.

"Where you supposed to land in Abuja, and have no passport or money?"

He was relieved. Apparently this happens all the time, and they have routines for it. They gave him a laissez-faire, checked him in at the airport hotel, clothed and fed him. And debited Ariks account. Then flew him back the day after.

GOAT ROBBS BANK

Following quotes are from the BBC, 23rd January 2009:

"Police in Nigeria are holding a goat handed to them by a vigilante group, which said it was a car thief who had used witchcraft to change shape.

A police spokesman in Kwara State has been quoted as saying that the "armed robbery suspect" would remain in custody until investigations were over."

The "armed robbery suspect" would be the goat.

KILLER PHONE NUMBER

BBC wrote about this as well. Rumors spread like wild fire that several people had died when they answered calls with the ID 09141. To the extent where the Nigerian authorities had to go reassure the public that this was untrue.

I changed the caller ID on one of my phones, so it showed that specific caller ID when I called my self, and then picked the call in front of my maid. She threw herself on the floor, crying, kissing my feet, and begging me not take the call.

I just looked at her and said "look at my Godlike powers, I will escape death", then I answered my own call.

Since then, she is terrified of me. She thinks I have special powers.

WE GET PLENTY MINERALS

The former minister of Energy got the following question in a TV-interview:

"What kind of minerals does Nigeria have?".

His reply? "We get plenty minerals, we get 7up, Pepsi, Cola".

Minerals means soft drinks in Pidgin. This is gold. The fact that he has no clue is fantastic.

BEING DEAF AND DUMB

One day, in Apapa, I was passing one of the beggars. They are difficult to notice as there are so many, but from time to time, someone catches your eye. He had a sign around his neck that said "I am deaf and dumb, please help me". So I ask him, "How u de bros? How bodi, na how much u de need?" His reply? "Oga a need plenty"

I gave him 5 quid. I mean the guy did not even bother to lie properly.

LETTER TO A EUROPEAN EMBASSY

This letter was sent to me from one of the Embassies. Basically it is a complaint for a denied Visa-application.

11-10-10

The Consul,

Embassy of ▮▮▮▮▮

Abuja

Dear Sir,

Re- Foremost, let me concede that I am clearly and fully persuaded about your right to refuse appeal to your decisions.

But permit me to place the following on record, for whatever it might be worth :

1. I, ▮▮▮▮▮▮▮▮▮▮▮▮, otherwise known as ▮▮▮▮▮▮▮▮▮▮, is a writer and publisher, privileged to be the winner of the prestigious Association of Nigerian Authors/Cadbury Prize 2004.

2. Having been a published writer and award-nominee since 1992, my works have been translated into German and Hindi by renowned international authorities.

3. Information about my person and accomplishments are verifiable and available in the public domain (internet).

4. For reasons personal to me, bothering on phobia, I have limited travel experience outside of Nigeria.

5. For reasons personal to me, I remain unmarried, with no apology for my decision.

6. I own and run an advertising firm and recently diversified into

publishing, with our books printed in UK and USA, and now UAE.

7. Pursuant to this new venture into publishing, we sought to utilize the opportunity offered by 2010 XXXXXXXXXXXX book fair, with focus on Africa to expose our works and buy books for our about-to-open bookstore.

8. I was not to be just a mere 'visitor', as insinuated, but the CEO of a publishing firm accredited as EXHIBITOR at the book fair.

9. We were commissioned, earlier this year, by the Lagos state government to produce 10,000 copies of my award-winning book : XXXXXXXXXXXX. (A rare honour).

10. My busy schedule apart, we could not conclude the travelling procedure to the US, as at the time I appeared at your mission, as we were yet to receive the foreword to the book being written by the Governor of Lagos State. That, we are honoured to have now received.

11. Same busy schedule, late receipt of hard copy of letter of invitation from XXXXXXXXXXXX, and difficulty of booking on your site led to my late appearance. (Pls recall I had earlier written in about this and called to explore the possibility of applying for XXXXXXXXXXXX visa from XXXXXXXXXXXX, as I had thought I would be able to go to XXXXXXXXXXXX before the trip to XXXXXXXXXXXX)

12. I was interviewed by a remarkably pleasant Lady, who took her time to go through my ton of documents and the books from our stables that I brought, before dashing back to the airport to catch a flight back to Lagos.

13. It is with bewilderment that I receive the news of a refusal of my application and the accusation bothering on fraud that "there is no proof of this money in any of your accounts".

14. It might interest you that I came in with statement of accounts from GT Bank and Ecobank. I tendered both. The lady exercising her wisdom,

I guessed, perused through the statement, detached the last page which reflected the N4 million deposit, and returned the voluminous statement to me. Suffice it here to state here that the N9.1 million(70% of the total sum of N13 million) was deposited into the same GTbank account (See attached), which was presented to her.

15. Bear also in mind that I equally presented our bank statement from Ecobank with a fixed deposit of N3.5 million, apart from letters of introduction from both banks.

16. This company, being only 2 years old, is putting its statement of affairs together. If we had been asked, we would have explained to you. But I came in with my personal income tax certificate.

17. To insinuate fraud, is pathetic. Would it not amount to sheer stupidity on my part to leave my thriving businesses in Nigeria, not deliver the commissioned books to Lagos state government, refuse to collect the outstanding sum of N3.9 million with the government, to go take up residence in XXXXXXXXXXXX? How low do we have to stoop?

18. We were bonafide exhibitors at the fair, paying for the stand and other expenses was a huge cost to our young organization, which we were eager to bear, to access the international market and hopefully make adequate returns from sales, while stocking our bookshop here.

19. What if I am unmarried and have no children? Must I marry? What if I have never travelled to Schengen area before ? Isn't there a first time? So much for stereotypes in the face of such highly regarded "Western values" of non-discrimination. When will you upgrade on these antiquated measurement tools that equate responsibility with marriage ? Not even your strange rules will make me compromise on my integrity.

20. I had very good impression of XXXXXXXXXXXX. My 2 Masters degrees – One in international law and diplomacy, the other in Political Science, I thought had prepared me well. My years of practice in journalism and broadcasting, I thought, taught me a few things. But

nothing beats a first-hand experience. Even if I had to fly from Lagos to Abuja to have it.

21. The shoddiness of your method, which leaves my passport in your custody for 2 weeks +, with my emissary repeatedly turned back, and the insinuation and accusation in your letter of refusal, stand however in sharp contrast to the warmth and gaiety of the lady who interviewed me, with her educated interest in books and writing.

22. I hold on to that as my lasting memory of an otherwise regrettable trip to the Embassy of XXXXXXXXXXXX in Abuja.

23. Thank you.

Sim

No Sim, we thank you, for this amazing complaint.

CONDUCTING A NIGERIAN MEETING (THE CORRECT WAY)

The overall protocol for meetings is to really exaggerate the participants and stakeholders. And by overdoing it I mean at least an additional 20-35 people present. It gives a sense of transparency which in turn gives a sense that corruption cannot fester. Of course, corruption takes place after the first meeting that drains any companies human resources, and that meeting is always between four eyes only. Opening prayers are as important as the meeting itself. Pray to as many Gods as humanly possible and that your schedule allows you to. Even if the meeting itself is about a robbery or a coup d'etat. God promotes ambition and results in Nigeria, not God causes per se.

1-Be grateful. First and foremost to the person that spoke before you, and the MC that gave you the floor. Thank them both. Make sure to face all directions and give your thanks multiple and repetitive times.

2- Respect the fact that people lied, stole, killed and broke the law to climb on the social ladder. Embrace the fact that you are lower in the food chain. Use titles like your life depended on it. Oga, Oga Madame, Chief, Dr, Master. When in doubt, always revert to Chairman. That title always works.

3- Appreciate the audience. Show it by emphasizing what privilege it is that you are invited to speak. Or even attend. Use words such as privilege, honor. Top op with adjectives. Rare honor. Etc.

4- Appreciate the value of the meeting itself. Once again, make it clear, that it is clear for you, that you will benefit from this get together. Thank and praise the people who arranged the meeting. Do not forget the host, and the people who owns the venue. Thank God. Thank everybody again on behalf of everybody, even if you don´t have a mandate to do so.

5- Respect the previous speakers. The best way to do that is to repeat what they said. It proves that you have been listening and not sleeping. It also gives the people that actually have slept the chance to catch up. Use referrals. "It is just as John said" and "I agree with the previous speaker". Then repeat what they said, with your own words. Do not put yourself on limb by adding new information. Those political risks are for white people.

6- Respect other people's time. Make sure to inform them of the same. Then, do the exact opposite. It´s totally appropriate to do so as long as you follow protocol. Then talk for hours.

7- Do not pass the floor on to the next speaker before summarizing what you have said. Once again, that gives the people who just woke up the chance to recap everything. It also bundles the information in a nice way for the next speaker, so he can take your summary and repeat it. It´s good manners.

8- Be sensitive to what is happening around you. If people are fainting, falling asleep and playing with their phones. Raise your voice, and use words as "as a final word", "before I take my seat as the rest of you" "the conclusion is". Then proceed talking for at least another hour.

9- All meetings are capped with a closing prayer. Once again, to an Orgy of Gods and religions. You never know who is listening.

LAST BUT NOT LEAST

I think this last story really embodies what I love about Nigeria. It represents the country at its core.

I was in my car, and all of sudden traffic stops. I kid you not, 50 people where fist fighting and another 300 was watching, but it was just a matter of time before they joined the action. I was in the middle of it, and had no clue how to get out of there as fast as I could.

So, I opened my windows. Put the volume in max, and choose a CD with Nigerian high-life. Within an instant, the fighting stops, everybody starts dancing instead, or at least moving their hips, the crowd disperse in different directions. And I can pass without any problems.

There you go, that is Nigeria for you.

THE 419'S-a travelogue about a country on crack

www.ingramcontent.com/pod-product-compliance
Lightning Source LLC
Chambersburg PA
CBHW020753230426
43665CB00009B/572